Uncovering the
the
I AM

Celebrate the Prodigal

Nan W. Burke

BALBOA.
PRESS
A DIVISION OF HAY HOUSE

Balboa Press books may be ordered through booksellers or by contacting:

Balboa Press
A Division of Hay House
1663 Liberty Drive
Bloomington, IN 47403
www.balboapress.com
1 (877) 407-4847

Because of the dynamic nature of the Internet, any web addresses or links contained in this book may have changed since publication and may no longer be valid. The views expressed in this work are solely those of the author and do not necessarily reflect the views of the publisher, and the publisher hereby disclaims any responsibility for them.

The author of this book does not dispense medical advice or prescribe the use of any technique as a form of treatment for physical, emotional, or medical problems without the advice of a physician, either directly or indirectly. The intent of the author is only to offer information of a general nature to help you in your quest for emotional and spiritual well-being. In the event you use any of the information in this book for yourself, which is your constitutional right, the author and the publisher assume no responsibility for your actions.

Any people depicted in stock imagery provided by Thinkstock are models, and such images are being used for illustrative purposes only. Certain stock imagery © Thinkstock.

Print information available on the last page.

ISBN: 978-1-5043-6098-2 (sc)
ISBN: 978-1-5043-6099-9 (e)

Library of Congress Control Number: 2016910873

Balboa Press rev. date: 09/22/2016

What people are saying about this book

Uncovering the I AM is the true story of a remarkable life. In her book, Nan reveals the power of honest self-observation, awareness, and eventual self-love. It is a testament as well, to the transformative nature of the healing modality of Reiki, and of the spiritual pathway in The Way of Mastery. Above all, it is a statement of the Love of which children remind us, and in so doing, help us retrieve the sense of innocence we think we have lost.

David Schock
www.daveschock.com
Senior Pathway Teacher

§

Nan captivates us in *Uncovering the I AM.* She invites us to share the transparency of her personal metamorphosis from dark, angry confusion to the joyful innocence of the child within. As one who wore a "coat of many colors," Nan shows us that we too can choose to transform ourselves. We too can loosen our grip on habitual patterns of self-judgment and misperceptions of ourselves and others. We can change a sense of personal unworthiness into a light-filled delight of self as the living Love and human face of the Creator here on this beautiful earth.

Read this book and find the joy of freedom in your journey as Nan did in hers.

Myra Partyka
Reiki Master Teacher
www.reikiworksri.com

§

In her book, **Uncovering the I AM,** Nan Burke opens her mind and heart to the reader in a way that at times is startling, yet is deeply refreshing. Nan shares openly her journey from fear, guilt, shame, and judgment, to joy, peace, contentment, and love.

While Nan's journey is uniquely hers, all those who read this book will benefit profoundly. Her transparent self honesty calls readers into their own deep self reflection. Nan's simple message is that anyone can change, no matter what has happened in their lives. She joyfully shares that if she can do it, so can you!

If you pick up this book and read it, your life will change. You will be invited and challenged to get real with yourself, forgive yourself, and ultimately, to love yourself unconditionally.

John Mark Stroud
Founder: *One Who Wakes*
www.onewhowakes.org

Acknowledgments

I offer heartfelt gratitude to Jeshua ben Joseph, (Jesus), Christed friend and teacher. He was a man who grew into and modeled for me, even up to his final breath, the realization that the moment-by-moment choice for love, can transform every fear-based expression. The same gratitude goes to Jayem, (Jon Marc Hammer), who served and learned as a Vietnam veteran and who since 1987, has selflessly channeled, discerned, spread, and lived the message of our brother, Jeshua, through the Way of Mastery works. Likewise, I embrace in warm HeartHugs the many kindred souls worldwide, who resonate within that message that, "only love is real."

I joyously give equal thanks to Dr. Mikao Usui, pioneer of the healing modality of Reiki, who appreciated that he was, as every being of all realms is, "the flow of life force energy." He recognized such energy as Love Itself, and spread the message of compassion through the practice of Reiki, the "spiritually guided life force energy." The same gratitude goes to his selfless protégé, Myra Partyka. As Reiki master teacher to thousands, she daily attunes herself to the Christ View, that we are in essence, innocence and compassion, embodied in the Reiki principles as offered by Dr. Usui,

The four of you, and every brother and sister of whatever spiritual persuasion, who honors self, and who lives out a heart-centered awareness of love, have by your own healing, made me more aware of my wholeness and freedom. Thank you.

Continued blessings …

To Audrey and Victor:

May you ever be, within your hearts
the sweet children who taught me to find again, and
to free from powerlessness, the child within me.
Together, we laugh and play, clap and dance, rest in silent wonder,
and greet each moment
with awe and joyful innocence.
Thank you.

Table of Contents

Foreword

Did you notice? You have a precious jewel in your hands ... right now!

I have known Nan Burke for a number of years. I have watched her in the cauldron of group processes at my workshops and pilgrimages. She was always willing to reveal what has been concealed, to seek not escape, but a deeper understanding of her personal patterns. In this humility, she especially expanded her capacity to enfold every experience in the loving womb of a very real palpable forgiveness.

But more than this, I have been blessed and privileged to feel her hold an audience in the palm of her hand and move those folks from laughter to tears, from hesitation to inspiration, and most of all, to look within honestly at the places where fear may yet have been keeping house, and allow it to be dissolved into a present love.

She does this not as some skilled speaker or facilitator extraordinaire, much less by any trace of a desire to so captivate them. Rather, the miracles occur because of her extraordinary offering of *utter transparency*. Nan models then, the most essential quality that allows us all to embrace our humanity in the love of our shared and eternal spirituality: light dissolves darkness every time if given half a chance! Her unpracticed humor comes from this transparency, and with it always comes insight, like pearls on a string that you too, can add to as you journey with her through this, her first book, ***Uncovering the I AM***.

We learn and unfold from those who have sincerely made the trek from fear to love, who have lived in the tumble dryer of our lives' unfoldings and yet have found a way to turn the mind back upon itself looking intently and curiously at that life, until the deepest reasons for events unmask themselves in revelation, and even mystical awakening.

In this then, I see and honor Nan as Crone, Way-shower, Teacher, and an always humorous Friend of the Heart we all share.

Journey with her, dear reader, and breathe deep. Pearls await for the string of your own journey. Savor every paragraph like a fine vintage wine, and let it breathe in your own deep breath, so the flavor of her sharings may suffuse every cell. And when you are done, put it down, then pick it up later, and read it again. I promise you yet more pearls will appear right before your eyes. The journey of healing into Love's Reality has a depth that requires our care, our patience, and just a smidgen of our willingness.

Streams of Joy,

Jayem

www.wayofmastery.com

Chapter One

Affordable Psychotherapy

2010 - Wakefield, Rhode Island

Gerald and I, strangers until today, face each other as instructed, seated on the wooden floor holding each other's forearms and with my legs straddled across his so we can gaze into each other's eyes. Naturally graying hair and deep furrows in his forehead make Gerald seem older than his 76 years. I, at 67, claim the saving grace of a bottled blonde, but I sport laugh lines and similar creases. We are the oldest among the ten people at the wellness center in this one day retreat focusing on honest self-inquiry.

We two stare into one another's eyes, as the moderator purrs, "Tell your partner of some transgressions or omissions in your life that you truly regret. Just state it, 'I acknowledge that I threw the baby out with the bathwater, and I forgive myself.' No explanations, no details; just say it, plain and simple. And feel it, folks, truly mean that forgiveness part. Your soul is asking this of you." She adds, "The listener waits, but asks no questions in response to the acknowledged act or omission. It's the forgiving yourself that's the biggie here."

"And you listeners give eye contact and empathetic listening to your partner. Be absolutely present to him or her. If you truly want your money's worth out of this day, you'll each let your psyche push out of you whatever it is that's loitering inside."

The other couples haven't started yet, so Gerald jumps in first. After speaking, he seems genuinely consoled and relieved at having voiced to me his lifelong penchant for giving in to the insistence of others in order to gain approval or keep the peace. I am glad for him, silently noting the serenity he exudes.

The rest of the folks are still dickering over who goes first, so I blurt out to Gerald, "I betrayed my religious vows as a nun in a two-year affair with another nun, and I forgive myself." Shock widens Gerald's eyes, but I plunge forward, "I acknowledge that I humiliated and hurt adolescent children as a teaching nun, physically beating them with a steel ruler, and I forgive myself."

Verbally vomiting, I continue, "I forgive myself for being too fearful of living alone, so I sought out my partner in Old San Juan, after he deserted me on the island of Culebra. I forgive myself for living with him in a cockroach-infested back room instead of admitting error of judgment to my family." Gerald's eyes blink and flicker, but he instantly recovers. I mutter, "Then, against all reason, I married him. Wow! And I forgive myself for that!"

By now Gerald is rocking back and forth slightly on his haunches but to his credit he has not faltered in his empathetic stare. I am energized by these admissions and Gerald's painfully steadfast expression, so I hurtle onward, "... I shot those sick, helpless dogs, and I forgive myself." I tack on, "... and drowned those kittens at the dock." There is only a tightening of Gerald's fingers on my elbows as I rush into a litany: "... I tossed that injured puppy into a plastic bag and hurled it into the bay in the dark of night and I put down my three faithful dogs rather than allow my soon-to-be ex-husband to threaten me with hurting them. And I forgive myself for dumping their bodies in an open field." Gerald's fingernails now painfully dig into my elbows, but I can't stop the projectile gushing of words, so I throw in, "...I borrowed my friend's husband to father a child for me, and I forgive myself." Gerald's body noticeably sags. It goes limp when I tag on, "And I forgive myself for leaving my two year old baby girl sleeping in my car when I went in for a tryst with Violette, one night."

Couples are still talking, so I stick on, "Then, back in the States, I shot my noisy rooster, to please my bisexual partner and I forgive myself. I sold my soul to her, actually. Yep, I forgive that too."

Other transgressions bubble to the surface, the S&M stuff, the credit cards bills, the screaming arguments in front of my daughter, but there is no time for me to include them, as the moderator calls the group to reconvene. This is merciful, because Gerald's composure has crumbled. He is cooked, shell-shocked. He probably never processed the last couple of admissions.

We return to our own backrests on the polished wood floor. I rub the indentations on my forearms where Gerald's grip has left purpling bruises. Gerald has not made eye contact with me since the mention of the "husband borrowing," and Violette's "tryst."

When the retreat ends, I help put things away and don't see Gerald again. I doubt I ever will, presuming that from his view, he's heard the confessions of a religious nutcake, bisexual serial animal killer, hiding in Rhode Island. I smile inwardly at the scenario of Gerald fearing he'll see my photo on an internet *Wanted* site and that his conscience will drive him to turn me in and be a witness at my arraignment.

I, though, can drive home in light-hearted peace, having finally begun to uncover the cesspool of guilt that has festered in my soul for years. I had just voiced, in laundry list fashion, various acts of mindless violence. I heard these actions in their raw ugliness, voiced them and saw horror in the eyes of a listener. I had admitted to arrogant disregard for the sanctity of life - both of animals and humans. I had faced the shame of ownership, without the softening of any explanation or mitigating circumstances.

This stream of confessions surprised me with its ferocity as it heaved from my depths. It was grace in action. I had finally begun to honestly view my past, to claim it, as the mosaic of my own personal choices. I saw with searing clarity that the offensiveness I had openly or furtively aimed at others, basically sprang from my need for outward control because within there was only chaos, not a shred of recognition that there was anyone *in there*.

Chapter Two

Indwelling Truth Inches Forward in the Eternal Now

These things happened. I invite you to consider the possibility that I chose every minute of my life in order to mirror to me the illusion that I was unloved, unsafe, and unworthy. Could it be that as pure spirit, emanating from the Mind of an all-loving God-Source, I chose to incarnate as a human with those particular vibratory fields? I did not send forth these energies consciously at first. In the womb and as a newborn and infant, I definitely shared in the dissonant energies around me, but I was relatively swaddled in the newly-created's innate knowledge of its perfection and innocence. I was aligned and connected to my LoveSource. Soon though, even before a passing year I would begin to relinquish that awareness of connection. I could never truly *be* disconnected from ParentSource, the uninterrupted flow of unconditional Love. But I would learn quickly that my surface wellbeing lay in the conforming to the conditions presented to me for the display of love as reward. I would let go of the certainty of divine Love, in whose image and fullness I am eternally sprung forth and would seed secret fears within my own psyche, falsely assuring myself that I could only find safety, security, and love outside myself. I then mastered the human art of fashioning experiences that "proved" those secret fears to me.

How do I know this? I don't. That is, I don't know it with the mind. The mind creates structures of, "I should, I musn't, I'm not there yet, I can't, I need to, etc." which spring from comparison and lack. This is the world speaking. No, I have discovered a knowing that is heart-centered. I listened to the heart. I discerned a vibrant joy and an expansion that emanates when the mind is quietened. The heart does not filter things through interpretation, as the mind does. The heart discerns the inner voice of connection. When I found the courage to allow myself to truly feel and value that inner voice, peace came. A growing awareness of connection to my Source aligned and harmonized within me. A knowing calm and a childlike trust began to suffuse me daily, and I continued to listen to the heart. When the ego-mind, which is only a human substitute for God, brought back the fears and threats of consequence that the world of power had fostered within me as a child, I would return to the heart's knowing of peace, safety, and joy. The heart was able to allay the fears, calm the doubts. This was a process. I rediscovered a lightening and an unburdening. It was a sovereignty of the true freedom of my birthright within existence.

This book is a personal archaeological dig, in which I excavate my way through what I once saw as the sewers of my life. Under a seemingly respectable, yet adventuresome surface, spanning over seventy years in New York, Puerto Rico, and the Hamptons, I hid the festering detritus of a soul in distress.

How does the caterpillar know when to start spinning its cocoon? What signal does it heed to barricade itself within its self-made coffin, only to emerge totally, alchemically transmuted? I followed that same instinct as I paid attention to the dim, but persistent urgings of my heart, to remove myself, body and soul from a dead-end. Like the caterpillar, I dissolved the personas I had accumulated. I self-liquified, emerging from a dark stillness able to love. I underwent a process of complete meltdown and rebirth when I fled to Rhode Island, beckoned by Audrey, an as yet unborn child, who would teach me my innate beauty, as I would hers.

When my soul knew I was desperate enough to listen to an inner voice of innocence and to grow in awareness of Truth, my soul showed me how to forgive self for its misperceptions of virtually everything. I grew towards finally recognizing my individual frequency within the harmony of the Creator's gift of free will. This is a mysteriously prodigal gift. It does not need my approval to organically unfold its God-Self magnificence in and as individualized, authentically sovereign human beings. We humans are freely given freedom. We are freely gifted the will to choose anything. Each of our souls knows how and when we will awaken from the illusory dream of disconnect. Each soul knows that its human form will be suffused once again in heart, mind, body, and spirit with the *knowing* of our own true nature as the perfectly whole and inseparably unblemished child of God.

Butterfly emerging from chrysalis. (Sketch by Gisela Brogi)

God is nothing if not everything. God (or whatever word we choose to conceptualize the Nothing and Everything) does not judge Itself. God is not, "out there." There is no, "out there." God is Life's pulsing. God is Truth's vibration. God is Love's harmony. And every creature of every potential realm exists resonating with its own frequencies within that Eternal Song of Love. We humans seem to be the only ones who question that harmony. When we judge anyone, ourselves included, we tell God-Self, "You didn't get this one right!" God is *unconditional Love*. Conditions are a human invention of time and space, and throughout my life I habitually agreed to love, "*... on condition that ...*"

However, eventually, like the caterpillar, I inched my way toward unraveling the tapestry of my individual patterns of behavior. I found the roots of my choices, skewed as they were by my misperceptions which in themselves sprang from my soul's particularly chosen fields of vibrational human energy. In gut wrenching, soul searing episodes of layered insights, I saw with horror my lifelong blindness to others' uniqueness. I stared directly at my arrogant disregard for the cherished sovereignty of every individual. Because I did not know there was anything beautiful within me, I never recognized innate beauty in others. At last, I truly began to *listen* to the echoes of what my soul, my heart, and all creation had always tried to show or tell me.

In these pages I consider how, as pure Consciousness, I chose to enter into humanity within the fabric of a particular family with its myriad generations passing along DNA-infused attitudes, conventions, norms, and secret fears. I explore to the roots of my personal patterns admitting to how I identified with and acted out age old delusions. In such exploration I discovered that a lifetime of apprenticeship to energies driven by fear can still eventually explode into a mastery of self forgiving and a moment-by-moment awareness of the mystery of innocence. And in that discernment, I saw that I had played too seriously with those fear-based energies. As every human does, within the unconditional allowance of the divinely given gift of free will, I got so caught up in the play that I forgot it was a game that I as sovereign being could script and dream as if it were real.

I share a way through the maze. I see that we are, in Oneness, the God-Self. We are Love's Light but in the power of free will's game choice, we fabricate comparison. We take seriously the masks of violence, pride, guilt, and anger with which we voluntarily cloak ourselves to hide the possibility that we could be shimmering in the magnificent power of being. I own up to wearing those disguises of apologetic smallness and I am now lovingly, gratefully permitting them to dissolve.

Come see how - only when I was humanly ready to - I surrendered the fear-filled "me" I thought I was, to the ongoing process of living *as* the Love and Light of the pure spirit, the soul I AM. Witness how I awakened from victim-based defensiveness into the timeless joy of allowing my pure Beingness to "Take Me with You to Where I AM."

Hooked on the Human Coat Tree

"Hooked on the Human Coat Tree" (Sketch by author)

Chapter Three

Hooked on the Human Coat Tree

I recently had a mental picture of myself as a human coat tree. There I was, in a lifelong, "poor me," pose, swirling around with all those whom I thought had "victimized" me. My parents, teachers, colleagues, and a lifetime of folks hung off me, helplessly hooked where I had vengefully attached them. We waltzed and spun in the macabre grip of a gruesome energy that I alone had consciously concocted.

I decided, in that gifted moment of insight that it was time to let them all "off the hook." It was time to free them and me, and any other beings with whom I had ever interacted, of any blame whatsoever. I saw that no one was at fault for who I had become. No one was guilty of failing to measure up to my expectations. No one had failed to see my world through my filters, just as I could never see through theirs. Not they, nor any teachers or authorities, religious or governmental systems, not anyone or anything had ever caused my life to turn out one way or the other. And they, in truth had no idea that they were "hooked" anywhere. It was my own vengeful delusion

As much as my mind and ego protested it, my heart's *knowing* saw this Truth: *in the mystery and the flowering of Divine potential within free will, I, as every other human being, had freely chosen to place myself in each and every moment of my unfolding.*

There was a time when that idea turned my stomach and assaulted my "intelligence." It is common knowledge, is it not, that the world's changing tides sweep us up and turn our worlds upside down? Are we not products of our parents' and families' input and conditioning? Yes, but each of us is solely responsible for how we choose to filter each occasion, how we choose to react to circumstance, and whether we seek within or outside of ourselves for the happiness that seems obliterated. I saw that each of us, as pure spirit before we incarnate, chooses to play with particular and definitive human consciousness-generated energies. We choose to incarnate into families and cultures which pattern those energies. Then as we incarnate we lose sight of the "playing," and the "what if," part and fuse to a human body-mind identity with those energies running us, forgetting the game aspect. We forget that we can never be separate from the Love that eternally allows us the sovereignty to play the game. We become serious in our fear and self protectiveness. We attach ourselves to what we value and we value, above all, the need to be right.

And what do we want to be right about? Is it the "uh-ohs" that were planted by structures of authority, ideas cultivated by the world of striving and expectation? Or are we willing to allow a tiny feeling of relief that we could safely trust in a loving ParentSource who shared itself AS each of us, equally, fully, perfectly, and inseparably whole? Can we risk feeling in our hearts that each of us as pure spirit dared, from any of the mysteriously immeasurable realms of creation, to choose the daunting experience of being a human whose powers include making fears seem real and building worlds of thought which reflect that false reality?

Grace however, is what turned *me* inside out and swept my arrogant mind clean of its need to be "right." When I began to let go of each layer of supposed unlovable-ness, I knew that I felt sadness and guilt at my very core. I recognized that I had to eventually *truly* forgive myself for my expectations of others and for my judgment of self. My heart knew that my perceptions were skewed and that *self-forgiveness and allowance of an innate vastness of consciousness and beauty were the keys to peace.*

I experienced a late-onset eyesight challenge. Decreasing depth perception, blindness within glare, and actual blind spots striating both eyes, have all shown me physically, that perceptions deceive. In certain lighting my eyes play tricks and I now "see" things that are not there, and literally trip over and bump into things that are indeed in front of or beside me. This *retinitis pigmentosa* condition helped to jump-start the grateful process of heart-knowing transformation. This gift of a vision struggle, in turning my physical world into "smoke and mirrors," has made me realize that every perception I have ever had, of anyone or anything *and* the mental constructs I fashioned from those misperceptions, *and* my actions or omissions that have resulted from those attitudes, have all been delusional.

In the, "Human Coat Tree" scenario, I tried to recall every person I had ever blamed for a particular grievance in my life. I looked them in the eye, thanked them for the "dance" we had shared, and unhooked them from the false time-lock in which my perceptions had stubbornly placed them. In the moment I unhooked each person, I forgave myself my secret fears regarding them, and I freely chose to admit that there was no way I could ever have really known what their secret fears were. The frightened child within me who had at one time sought their approval or applause began to grow more comforted as she let go her grip on a sense of sad powerlessness. I grew lighter and more expansive as I unhooked each person, and eventually was truly filled with a palpable joy and the deepest sense of heartpeace.

This grace-filled insight removed a major obstacle to my healing. My heart swelled with humble gratitude and my spirit soared in renewed awareness of the harmony embedded within the Divine's gift of free will. In this gesture of gently lifting every being off the various hooks where I had placed them, I was graced with the heart-felt knowing that every one of us human beings is joyously sovereign and free to "show up" as and how we choose. I recognized that living in this spirit of allowance would be a major step in healing my broken sense of self. I would allow myself to receive love in whatever form it appeared, even if I could not perceive it at that moment as love. I agreed to the "Is-ness" of everything, within the timeless, incomprehensible mystery of this gift of free will.

Watercolor abstract, "Self-Erected Walls." (14" x 17") by author in 2008.
Private collection (Photo by Carol Larkin)

Chapter Four

Poised at the Maze Entrance

Take Me with You, to Where I Am is a venture into a self-constructed maze. I emerged from it into an awareness of a God-Self, a personal worth hidden within the hell of countless obstacles set up by my own lifelong self-defeating, erroneous perceptions. I gradually grew into a willingness to tear down the defensive battlements around my heart. I chose to not erect more walls of fear but to remain open and vulnerable to the possibility that I could be lovable. I felt into the possibility that I could have been created by a Love that shared Itself fully AS me and AS all creation. I surrendered to the growing awareness that I actually *was* Truth, and Life, and Love in human form. I recognized, and invited the divine within me, to lovingly dispel any latent distress or alarm my mind associated with meeting the God of my childhood. I permitted myself to let go of the mind's perception of a God who watched, and counted, and judged, and compared. My heart began to know that during this lifetime and when I take my last breath, the only changes to "meeting" God will be on my part, that is, my mind's part because I came to know that I *am God, I am Life itself.* I humbly acquiesced to the dawning reality that *everything is God and that there is nothing outside of me.* I gratefully acknowledge the mystery that I am the created child of a divine ParentSource who has rapturously shared Itself AS me. I confessed to myself that I would rather be cherished and thus comforted by an inner heartpeace than to continue listening to others' voices in my head and to be right about my being judged.

My soul took me with it through this maze to discover the treasure of the Truth: *I am Home.* Soul led me to remember that *never could I ever have left Home.* True Home is the unconditional Love in which I am, as spirit, eternally birthed. True Home is the moment-by-present-moment, rebirthing of Self in this earthly life. It is a Home-Love from which I can never separate because the Source-Home-Love, shared its infinite potential as creation, as me. Admittedly I stay joyfully vigilant in this process of moment-by-moment choosing to recondition myself. I am human. I have developed habits to which I often default. Humans have emotions which spring up, feelings which deserve to be felt into and finally allowed to dissolve … with no self-recriminations. They are to be innocently witnessed, with wonder and curiosity … and then permitted their transmutation into the Love's potential from which they sprang. This is an on-going process. It involves the breath, a willingness to deeply feel your emotions back to their source in your very cells. It requires a growing awareness of inherent innocence. And it results in eventual compassionate self-forgiveness and gratitude to your soul that you chose to prodigally utilize the ineffable gift of free will.

ᏆᏨᏆᏨ ᏆᏨᏆᏨ ᏆᏨᏆᏨ ᏆᏨᏆᏨ

I state here that there was a period in my life, between the ages of 27 and 65 that I would have bristled and squirmed at the mention of 'Jesus.' I would have ceased reading or listening. I have come to understand that my skewed judgment of this man called Jesus (the Greco-Roman form of his native Aramaic Yeshua ben Youssef) was a result of the erroneously exalted ideas associated with him by the world's various religious beliefs. I do not 'believe' anything about the man. I 'feel' in my being that he humanly discovered that Love was the source of all Being.

Religions seem to be groups of people with similar 'beliefs' about what God is, or what they hope God is. Spirituality seems to be a one-to-one relationship with a God-Self within one's being, and which is expressed naturally and effortlessly by all creatures, animate and inanimate, in every realm throughout all creation. We humans seem to need to question it and tag it as something to be strived for.

I have finally grown comfortable with every one of my life's choices and have allowed a self-love to blossom. I did this with the help of the fellow named Jesus, or Jeshua, who considers himself brother and equal and whose life was an example to me of spirituality and soul expression. He was not a Christian, nor am I. Neither was he a religious leader. He just followed his heart's discerning, and people followed him. But he grew into a christedness, that is, an anointing or celebrating of the heart's knowing that only Love is real. I too am growing into that christedness of mind and heart.

My heart's peace nestles in a knowing of this Love which he tried to communicate by his life of increasing awareness, and by the extending of a message. His voluntary death within excruciating circumstances, demonstrated his realization that a body can undergo any form of physical and psychological pain and still answer each of those assaulting moments with love's intention and extension. He was not a victim. He was not sacrificed to expiate sin. There is no sin. There is only fear and the illusion of separation. This was his life's message: Love can overcome fear. Love can trump death. He lived that message until he chose to take his last breath.

His body, and mine and yours are a communication device for extending within time, the timeless truth that there is no victimhood. There is only the freely chosen savoring of any and every flavor of vibratory energy, love-based and fear-based, in order to eventually transmute them into this Truth that only Love is real. It is this Love through which I now joyfully live, breathe, and function as a human being. In a growing awareness of everyone's never-lost innocence, I delight in Jeshua's invitation to love my neighbor as myself. I savor the opportunity to love my enemy because my only enemies are the very thoughts I myself create within my skewed perceptions that there could possibly be separation. I love those thoughts as my creations, forgive myself for their springing forth from habits, and bring them back into the innocence from where they came. I continually invite myself to cultivate the ability to experience every potential extension of the God-Self unfolding Itself as neutral occurrences. I try not to answer violence with returned violence, anger with more anger, nor complaints with my own complaining ... even if I disguise them as observations. I extend love and forgiveness to myself for reacting to whatever word, gesture, act, omission, or occurrence I perceive, whether that be from individuals, governments, cultures, or in the media, or the weather, predicted or not. That is the christedness of mind and heart that brings Light to our world's perceived darkness. That is the Jesus I know and thank. I walk in his energy and example, and with those throughout history' ebb and flow who also learned to live that Way.

ෂ෨ෂ෨   ෂ෨ෂ෨   ෂ෨ෂ෨   ෂ෨ෂ෨

Chapter Five

A Signpost in the Maze

The book's subtitle, ***Celebrate the Prodigal***, explores who might be the real prodigal in Jesus' story of a rich, loving father and his two sons. Jesus told the parable simply, but it is pregnant with applications to each human's personal journey of reclamation.

Jesus (*Jeshua ben Joseph*) told of a son who demands his inheritance from a rich father, then puts great distance between himself and his home. He spends freely, until famine drives him to be a pigsty boy in a strange land. In guilt-laden wretchedness, he wends his way "home," willing to grovel before his father for mercy. As the son approaches the homestead, *before he can even begin to utter his prepared speech for pardon, the father runs out to him,* sweeps him into a loving embrace, and orders the household to immediately prepare a feast of joyous celebration.

The son never gets to utter a word of remorse. Moreover, the father gifts him with sandals, a new robe, and a ring, celebrating a son's willingness to re-turn home. There is never a word of reproach, not one reference to judgment or pardon. It seems there is nothing to forgive. There is only a father's delight and a recognition that the son was never absent from the parent's constant love. It is the celebration of a child's guiltlessness.

Gone from the son's consciousness is any shred of terror. He no longer feels fearful of judgment, from his father, from his brother, or from anyone in the household. He enters his homecoming, awakening from his self-made nightmare of supposed separation.

Implicit in the story however, now that the "lost" son realizes he could not have been truly distanced from his father's loving presence, is an understanding that he can begin to mend the rift that his actions created.

It is not the journey *to* the kingdom, but the journey *within* the kingdom of Love, that is the challenge for that son, and for us as humans.

The younger son has now been impacted by the full measure of the father's unconditional love. He has been honored for prodigiously, or prodigally, utilizing the father's eternally renewed, unconditional largess. He has been celebrated for recognizing that he had not been acting through love and has turned back to his Source. He cannot change the older brother's perspective, or alter his brother's jealously self-righteous rage and refusal to join in the father's celebration. But the awakened child-heart now has the privilege and responsibility to joyously, *in imitation of the father's unconditional welcome,* extend that love to his brother, and to all creation.

The older brother struggles with the fact that he, unlike his brother, stayed home and did not demand and spend. The father tells him, however, that he could have. Could this imply that he too has been prodigal, in its sense of miserly and guardedly wasteful? The father says that the riches are never-endingly his also. So, was that brother also prodigally wasteful in not seizing opportunities to generate exploratory experience for himself? He too, could have guiltlessly spent freely of his father's gifts. All he had to do was live out his free will, but he acted from a perspective of scarcity and fear of loss. It was his own choice to stay and not expand his opportunities.

As the father does not fault the younger son the free expression of his sovereign right to claim his birthright of free will, so does he extend to the other son the sovereignty to act authentically at the homestead. Both sons can unfold in their own ways within Love's infinitely prodigal potential.

These sons used their power to construct a framework of reference within illusion. The younger dreamed he was distanced from Home. The older stayed home but dreamed of his righteousness and the "wrongness" of his brother's actions. Both sons conceived the illusion of comparison and guilt, projecting it on either the self or the "other."

The father does not judge either. He prodigally, beyond any "normal" range of generosity, allows the dreamer to unfold within the riches of free will, i. e., freely given infinite choices because he knows that every child mysteriously and timelessly harmonizes its way Home. That is Love's divinely orchestrated prodigality. The prodigal is celebrated. We, along with Jeshua ("*Ye-shua," the way-show-er)* can now live among our brothers with joyous, awe-filled thanks, loving one another. Relationship, the moment-by-moment interaction among all living beings, is the means through which Love expresses its prodigality. Let us all, each of us, be prodigal in the finest, fullest sense of the word.

Chapter Six

The Maze in Constant Construction

As a human, I ceaselessly unfold my talents as a complete production company in a life-long personal film industry which leaves Hollywood, Bollywood, and any wannabees behind in the cosmic dust. In any given instant, from birth to death, I am novelist, screenwriter, crew and cast. Timing my entrances and exits for optimal effect, I exploit circumstances as I play the hero, the villain, the gallant knight, or any toadie I want to be at any given moment.

As the scout, I orchestrate locations for my own benefit. By constantly morphing furtive manipulation of the scene, either in my mind or in actual circumstances, I illustrate, create special-effects, and am my own stuntman, seeking to look good in others' eyes. Once I sense approval, I think I have earned the right to be loved. As director, editor, dubbing expert, distributor, and theater owner, I attempt to control every aspect of what I see as my life's production and how I want others to perceive me.

Desiring total control, I am the projectionist, the stage and the screen itself, and the usher. I even stock and service the concession stand to be sure everyone seems satisfied. I engineer everything in my efforts to win safety and security. I sit in the audience as viewer, heckler, and film critic, skewing facts and coloring the outcome to my expectations. I constantly hold Academy Awards, and I sweep "Best" in every category.

I generate the whole enchilada of my "story". In the mysterious ebb and flow of Divine harmony, I also innocently "show up" in other's stories, in the age-old arising and passing away of history. God sees it all as Itself unfolding, "... and God saw that it was good." (Genesis 1:31)

God, as the parable's prodigally generous father, is the Fountainhead, a Daddy-Mommy Lovebucks, bankrolling my ability to produce this entire illusion of separateness. After all, God has the final word because, "In the beginning was the Word, and the Word was with God, and the Word was God." (John 1:1) I am birthed in and as this Word-Love, and as a loving, loved, and lovable being I will eventually awaken to that awareness of God-Self.

Incidentally the tale of the prodigal, or "lost" son, was supposedly one of the last parables Jeshua shared before he went up to Jerusalem to set into motion the steps leading to his death. This was his self-generated demonstration of how the constant choice for love can dissolve the effects of any action springing from fear. It was a searing energetic marathon of love's endurance he chose to undertake. But Jeshua had schooled himself in the constant awareness of the illusion of anything *but* love.

The night before he died, he passed through his ring of fear in the olive garden in Gethsemane. In the momentary grip of enormous fear, he sweated blood, begging that things be different. But when he dropped back into the his practice and choice of a heart-knowing trust, he could see with awe the power we humans have in making fear seem so real. He could see the cosmic joke we play on ourselves. His focus was likely on inwardly yet ecstatically laughing his way through those last hours. His body underwent what we see as excruciating torture and brutally degrading humiliation, but he knew it as bodily change, involving horrendous pain but not suffering. He knew that suffering is seated in attitude. He was voluntarily undergoing the culmination of his life's production: the proof that only Love is real. The body could be pained and destroyed but it was not his identity. He would prove, in resurrection that its form as body was merely a dense coalescence in-formed by the Light of pure spirit. Death was not existent as an ending. He would reappear as the vibrant Light in which he, and we, are created as spirit. Afterwards, he would ratchet down the vibratory energy of the Light to the frequency which each witness could tolerate. But he would prove that love is the only answer to violence in any form, physical emotional, or mental.

As human beings, each of us is all three of the parable's main characters. As the younger son, we ventured forth from a heavenly home as spirit, into a chosen self-made worldly hell of perceived distance from Love-Home. As the tale's older son also, we developed, and stubbornly resisted changing from, lifelong habits of resentful self-righteousness. And as the father whose riches are never ending, freely and equally shared, we have the power to choose to enter our own treasure house, our worth, our Comforter Within, the indwelling God-Self that we are. There we find the endless wealth of the Truth that we thought had eluded us. We find that we are Life itself.

Now in my seventies, I am experiencing a heartfelt celebration of a homecoming to self-worth. I live in self-acceptance. Laughingly recognizing when I fall back into my habitual patterns of fear, I can gratefully admit that I am a master of the innocent art of illusion.

All ascended beings - those who have, through love's expression, raised their vibratory frequency back to its original wholeness - all these heavenly hosts celebrate my willingness to explore my human potential, to discover what is fear-based and illusory, and to grow in expressing only love-based thoughts and deeds. Source knows all events are neutral, no matter what my inner critic writes in review. And I may have written my script as a drama involving mystery and sci-fi adventure, but God-Parent-Source knows that the only genre is comedy. All creation celebrates my sovereign use of its gifted power of free will. Love knows with certainty that eventually I will remember who I am and my "production company of one" will begin to proclaim glad tidings and great cheer, aware of being cherished and innocent, and living the Oneness of Truth.

Segment I

1942 – 1961

Heavenly Knowing Fades to Forgetfulness

Chapter Seven

Apprenticeship in Illusion Begins

August 1942 - Greenwich Village, New York City

Born into Wartime Blackout

From the vast panoply of life's potential vibrations available to experience, I as sovereign consciousness, freely elected to spend a human lifetime becoming a master of the need for approval, and its spawn, anxious defensiveness and furtive manipulation. To ensure these vibrations, my soul made a contract to incarnate into the adrenal-suffused womb of a loving, but wearied mother. She herself had chosen to be the oldest of eight children. Worn out by the raising of seven siblings during the tumultuous eras of Prohibition and the Great Depression, her own choice of nine pregnancies took an additional toll on her.

To further bolster that vibratory field, I chose a father whose energies seemed to center around suppressing a merry wit in order to remain invisible and thus not susceptible to public scrutiny. His mother's brother, James J. ("Jimmy") Walker, had been the personable, flamboyant, mayor of New York City from 1926 to 1932. The effervescent "Beau James" was forced by the presidentially campaigning Franklin D. Roosevelt, to resign in disgrace because of corruption in "Jimmy's" administration. My father, who lived under "Uncle Jim's" care, since his own father had died when my dad was twelve, virtually went underground in self-assumed, vicarious disgrace. He was eighteen at the time, and had to drop out of Holy Cross College in Worcester, MA. His mother, the original Nan Walker Burke, whose name I bore, seemed, in my child's eyes forever angry at this turn of events. My father somehow kept his confused anger in check publicly, but unleashed it on my mother and us older three of his five children. Although his subsequent career as a trial lawyer, put my father in the public eye, his body language seemed obsequious and apologetic, continually ducking what he perceived as exposure to vindictive scrutiny.

I chose all the contingencies which flowed from this particular familial and cultural energetics make-up of my parents' situations. My four siblings picked their particular time frame in our family dynamics and thus their own personal journey. Four other pregnancies opted out of our family, for whatever their souls' purposes were.

My life as a defiantly agitated, furtively approval-seeking human began in August 1942, as my parents' fourth pregnancy. First-born, Mary, lived only one day. Then came Ginny, three years older than I. An April 1942 late-term miscarriage preceded me and four months later, the gestation I chose began. It was flooded by angst-driven hormones fueled by a mother's fear of another miscarriage and the possible death of a husband drafted into the U S Army Air Corps, after 1941's Pearl Harbor. As I shared my mother's endocrine flow in the womb, the massive flow of WW II troops dramatically increased, sending men to the Middle East, the Pacific arena, the Aleutian Islands, Panama Canal zone, clandestine forces to southwest China, and of course, the European invasion. My mother and I spent her fourth pregnancy sharing a continual state of wartime disharmony, immersed in a disquieted apprehension, both internal and world-wide.

Anxious agitation was not the only energy I elected to savor and allow to run me. Contrarily, I chose to be born into an ambience in which I could absorb the energy of commando-style, "jump first, grab the parachute later," attitude to life's opportunities. Throughout my life, I generally seemed to opt for experience, then let my gut tell me if it felt worthwhile to continue in it or to jettison myself and start anew. Planning rarely entered the picture. Bravado and gut led me.

After I was born into a wartime blacked-out Manhattan in May of 1943, we followed my father to his posting in 1944 at Barksdale Field, Louisiana, and lived until the end of the war, on the air base where the German and Italian POWs were maintained. There was constant, noisy military activity as the airfield trained replacement crews and entire aerial-battle units between 1942 and 1945. This emotional turmoil, coupled with the pervasive threat of my father's unit being activated for overseas duty, played havoc on my mother's nerves and thus, my sister's and mine. It also, contrastingly set the stage for my personal can-do, "brook-no-opposition," attitude toward adventure.

The end of WW II did not ameliorate the foreboding, however. It morphed into a sense of inadequacy, jealous comparison, and subsequently, covert manipulation. These were fueled by seething resentment, when my brother was born five years later, after two more late-term miscarriages between our births, and subsequently, two more siblings after us.

So, from the time I was ten months old, "Mommy" had been either pregnant, or in grieving depression, or at best, just desperately tired. All of the above made a potent cocktail of misperceived unworthiness and sadness from which I drank deeply. I drained each glass, continuously pouring myself more of that noxious brew, and eventually smashed that mind's eye cocktail glass in resentful, "poor me" anger towards any unsuspecting soul.

To this day, in times of stress, the witness inside me still notices big time, not just a gut-searing tightness of alarmed confusion, but an added flashing lights, bells, whistles, 'n' sirens-abounding desperate need to be noticed and included in a blanket of assured safety. And I do not just crave this stamp of approval and validated inclusion. No, no, no; I want accolades, parades, and showers of praise heaped upon me for being worthy of being counted in.

"Pleeeeeze, Mommy! Pick me up! Pick me up! Smother me with kisses, embrace me with tender recognition of my 'specialness' to you! Notice how precious and capable I am! Please, just notice me," has translated glaringly into most of my adult interactions.

My brother may have replaced me as the younger and most vulnerable, and as the Walker Burke name-bearer, but I did not easily relinquish my favored status. Having practiced my apprenticeship skills in developing falsely misconstrued abandonment, I declared my own war, replete with undercover strategies. Though drenched in an undercurrent of anxiety, my wartime identity grew deeper in its daring but sneaky activities, stronger in its survival techniques. I was an attentive student of the human drama, an able apprentice in fear-based illusion. My siblings and I may have struggled within the life choices our souls had made, but I seemed to aim my anger at each of them in different ways, depending on my misconstrued perceptions.

Observation

As far back as I can remember, I felt like an interloper, a pretender. At all the many family gatherings, my entire family thrived on the turn of phrase, the barbed witticism, or outright jest. All of that merriment was at someone else's expense. It was a verbal rapier thrust to the heart, a "slash and burn" method of cutting down the "enemy" to one's own perceived stature. It was a feast of judgmental, "us against them." I just presumed that if we did it habitually as a family, then everyone else was doing the same to us, if not in actions, then in intentional thoughts.

My father and his family and friends were lawyers, builders, engineering entrepreneurs, and writers. They downed more than their fair share of alcohol but were quiet party-ers. They were still emotionally enmeshed in the Democratic Party politics of New York City. Dad himself kept a low public and social profile. Lingering shame of Jimmy Walker's political disgrace still persisted in his demeanor. My mother's family meanwhile, eight married siblings and their exponentially increasing progeny, was always up for a good Irish bash of a party. Their ranks included engineers, journalists, Jesuit priests, and more lawyers. Every gathering provided ample discussion of widely ranging topics, and it was a spirited, "no holds barred" atmosphere of attack and retreat.

As a child, I absorbed these mannerisms and attitudes; I made them my own, but then I subconsciously applied them to myself. I presumed that everyone thought as we did and therefore everyone outside me was finding the chink in *my* armor too, as we did with others. If we joked and sarcastically dismantled someone's reputation, then it seemed that they were automatically doing the same with me. Subsequently, I twisted my pride into an offended, strike-first shrewdness and my need for approval into a secretive, never-be-wrong vigilance. In most photographs of me as a baby or young child, I do not smile. I seem truculent or pensive. I believe I developed a self-righteous combativeness even at that early age. I most certainly never admitted to mistakes or transgressions.

Living an apprenticeship in illusion, I willingly chose to act from that perspective of feeling judged and found unworthy. I jumped the gun on outside observers as I defaulted to self-identifying as untrustworthy or phony. I now own that recognition and it is that for which I ask forgiveness because it is that false perspective that spawned the actions which hurt so many throughout my life. I have gone inward, painfully and not without massive doses of anguish and tears and uncovered such a sense of powerlessness in the face of anger, and such a seething cauldron of unexpressed anger and subsequent sadness within myself.

I now know how I had coped as a child. My father harbored anger under his gentle demeanor, but in his humanness unleashed it periodically on my mother and on us, his children. However, we children were never permitted to express our own anger. Outbursts were not acceptable. Image was of utmost importance. Fear forged a steel-gloved hand of self-protection around my gut-heart and clamped off any expression of anger in rebuttal of a father's rage. As he unleashed his own powerless, unheard-child's anger and blindly directed it towards us, I coped as each of us humans does. The glove consequently walled in my heart and prevented it from feeling or expressing love's vulnerability. However, resentment invited me to express itself angrily outside the home as I unleashed my own fury on neighbors and playmates. In recent years, through living the practices of Reiki, through a self-balancing immersion into the Hawaiian attitude of Ho'oponopono, and through the Way of Mastery strategies of Radical Inquiry, innocence, and wonder, I have grown to see that steel glove as the inner child's powerful tool for survival. I have loved that protective glove, thanked it for its useful energy in preserving my heart, shielding it from assault. But I have loved it into acknowledging that it has also stifled my ability to express compassion. The glove's grip had choked off any voiced softness or tenderness of feeling. Anger had always bitterly followed upon annoyance.

I have thanked that glove, but even more to the point, I have admitted that it has always been *my own hand* within that glove, *my own hand* remained throughout my adult life, choking off any flow of love and compassion towards others. Aspects of me wanted to love, desired to be of service. But at the slightest trigger, the anger shot out because it had been clamped down and never allowed expression, never been acknowledged, never been acceptable. I looked with love on that energetic glove I had fashioned. Then I allowed it to dissolve into a revered and treasured artifact. It is a testament to the power of the Comforter Within. But it is not needed any more. Annoyance still arises, misperceptions continue to form, but the anger is dissipating. It has been uncovered and given its moment in the sun where the Light of Love is gradually dispelling it.

I have met and loved my secret fears. I have forgiven myself because I know in my heart that Love's ParentSource does not see transgression and does not judge. It loves *unconditionally* and so there is nothing within me that requires being forgiven. On my part, there is only the choice to let go of self-judgment and let go of the misperception that I could ever know what fuels the secret fears of anyone else.

In all of those formative years I grew increasingly fused to identifying myself as body. I humanly relinquished any Self-remembering as pure spirit, any echoes of shared Oneness in Pure Mind. And the more I identified as body-mind, the more deeply I ventured into victimhood and the "poor me" attitude, increasingly unaware of the God-Self as pure consciousness and choice.

Chapter Eight

Witness to the Maze

You are invited to read, skim, or skip the following vignettes. Whether you laugh or weep or if you think I dwell too much on the minutiae of days long past, know that I offer these "nanosecond glimpses" of my life to truthfully illustrate that no matter how circumstances seem to demonstrate otherwise, people *can change themselves.* In being transparent, I take the risk that you might find me despicable, loathsome, or pathetic. I probably seemed that way to those who were pained by my actions. Whether those folks were the intentional targets of my ire, mindless neglect, or intentional disregard, or the scandalized witnesses, they were nevertheless affected. Those people and creatures bore the brunt of my misperceptions which forged themselves into habitual attitudes and then detonated into repugnant actions.

I lived each of these episodes in my need to maintain control and to manipulate perceptions. I did it without looking at how it impacted others in life's rippling continuum. I continued to live and function in intolerable conditions because I feared losing the familiarity of what I had, even when I knew in my heart it was wrong of me and for me. I felt unworthy or incapable of rising to anything better and resentfully remained with the status quo. I became adept at life's seemingly "trade off" reality. I did not yet know that my Reality is Love in human form. Nor did I know that the purpose of my existence is to stay aware of my inseparable connection to Source and to extend Its love. I did not know love, did not feel worthy of being loved, and could not truly live love. The adage, "To thine own self be true," seemed to threaten me. To me, 'self' was an empty, meaninglessly unapproachable mystery.

I share with you that anyone can change. Grace and light are within us, are actually our essence as offspring of divine Self-Love. It does not seem evident in most of us or in the world's dramas because as vast, pure consciousness we each have elected to condense that God-Self into identifying as a body and "seeing" narrowly through two eyes.. The divine Source, the Parent, sees all its creations and Self-unfoldings only as whole, and only as brilliantly aglow with its own Light. What to us seems most dense or unconscious, or appears phony, unkind, severe, or even cruel and depraved, is equally loved and non-judged by God-Self, because the fear-based presumptions are instantly corrected by Love's Word. Free will continues eternally, organically revealing the infinitude of allowance and potential.

If you have anyone in your life who seems incorrigible like me, the person you will meet in these vignettes, do not despair. Do not place that person in a bubble of your own judgment, encasing him or her, never to be released. Recognize each person's own authenticity, even if it does not meet your biased expectations. Allow each person to "show up" just as he or she chooses to, in body form, in mannerisms and habits, and their influences or seeming lack thereof. If you want them to change, then first change yourself. Not one of us can change another. Each one of us is responsible for recognizing our own innate vastness while honoring the wholeness and inherent innocence of each of our brothers and sisters. In that recognition lies the secret of freedom. When each of us can allow our minds to quiet, and to choose instead to see guiltlessness in ourselves and others, healing happens. But the healing, the change, starts with the individual. It starts with self.

Forgive others their secret fears as you would have them forgive yours. Forgive yourself for your misperceptions, of what you "see" as their hidden, possibly fear-based motives. But especially, pray. Prayer is not petition, for then we would be thinking there is a power outside ourselves. As offspring of the Creator who has shared its fullness AS every created possibility, pray the conversation with Self who knows its Comforter Within. Utter a humble prayer of openhearted, unconditional love for yourSelf. Consider addressing your human self in the Ho'oponopono way of, "I'm sorry. Please forgive me. I love you, and I thank you." No analysis, no targeting, just give and receive it. Perhaps consider that you are addressing your small "me" and be sorry that you allowed fear to cause consternation and mental pain or physical discomfort for yourself. And in this recognition of your innate beauteous lovability, you cause your healing, your growth in awareness and will impact the consciousness of another being to cause its own healing. Change will happen, even if it remains hidden within the depths of each person's heart. It will come, even if it is not in this lifetime.

Someone must have prayed this way with me in mind.

Chapter Nine

The Apprentice Hones Her Skills

Early 1950's – Bayside Queens County, NY

Imposter

I received first and second degree burns on my face in a late summer, kitchen accident when I was an eight-year-old. Penicillin treatments and frequent bandage changing meant I missed the first six weeks of school. It was well into October when I was deposited at the office in the local Catholic school, told I was in Mrs. Hanson's 3rd grade class and escorted down the hallway to a classroom. A gray haired woman at the front kindly ushered me to a seat. For the next three weeks this woman repeatedly said things such as,

"*Mrs. Hanson* would like all of you to stand now."

"*Mrs. Hanson* does not want you to hand in papers without a name and date on them."

"Please draw a picture of the story's characters for *Mrs. Hanson*."

My apprenticeship in illusion was doing splendidly at this age, having developed tendencies to skulk and blend into the background if I felt intimidated. So I increasingly grew more fearful and sly, thinking that I was in the wrong classroom yet refusing to admit it to anyone. To my eight-year-old mind, this woman who constantly referred to the *Mrs. Hanson* in whose class I was supposed to be, could not possibly *be* that very same Mrs. Hanson. Why wouldn't she just say, "I," or "for me?"

Finally, two months later, another teacher came into the room and spoke directly to the woman, addressing her as, "Mrs. Hanson." It was not until then that I felt assured that I was indeed in the correct room. I had spent eleven weeks feeling unsafe, as a fake and an interloper, but stubbornly refusing to admit guilt or ask for help from other students or staff. I had automatically defaulted to a perception of self doubt and anxious fear that I would be "found out" as an imposter. Yet I was never going to admit to the frailty of being wrong. I was busy identifying as this body-mind and growing masterfully as an apprentice in the illusion of separation.

Implosion

In May of 1952, we moved from renting upstairs at the Mangano's house to our own home ten blocks away. We were now a family of four children. The baby, Rita, was just two-years-old and it would be another two years before Rosemary, the youngest of us five Burke children, would make an appearance.

The exciting move took place around my ninth birthday and I felt mixed emotions that in the disruption, my birthday party fell through the cracks. I felt gypped, yet relieved, because it side-stepped the inevitable clash of wills between my mother and me over my wearing some kind of party dress. I hated dresses, even as a toddler. I felt doubly uncomfortable in the vulnerability of bare legs and the imposition of frills and fluff. Not having a birthday party seemed like a fair trade-off in light of the exhilaration and adventure associated with the move to a new neighborhood. I especially liked being overlooked enough to be free to explore the acres of wooded paths and granite staircases of nearby Crocheron Park.

My friend, a year younger than I and frequent companion on the old block, often visited. One Sunday afternoon, we approached the access area near the public school. A plump, grey-haired old man sat on a stone bench and motioned us to sit down on either side of him. As we did, he put his arms around each of us. He slid his right hand inside my pants, his beefy fingers stroking my vulva and sliding down onto my vagina, one finger caressing my now awakened clitoris. It was a pleasant sensation. I didn't feel threatened or afraid, but I felt uncomfortable, because he was doing something to me that I knew was called, "private." and probably not done outside. I had pleasured myself that way and wasn't sure that someone else should be doing it to me. I did not stop him, even though I started to feel my parents would not approve of a stranger touching me like that. The man continued to stroke me and I wondered if he was touching my friend, the boy sitting at his other side.

He withdrew his hand and the three of us stood up. The entire time, not a word had been uttered. I reached out, took the man's hand and began to tug the three of us in the direction of my house. I prattled on, during the whole walk towards my street, with my friend chiming in occasionally. The stranger never said a word, though sometimes he grunted or nodded. Increasingly nervous, I stopped at the corner of my block, knowing instinctively not to let the old man know where I lived. He let go of our hands and without a word or a backward glance, continued walking further along the avenue. I stood waving good-bye, somehow relieved that the man never looked back. My friend and I did not talk to each other on the way down the block to my house. When his father came to pick him up, he didn't say good-bye. I never saw him again.

Even as a nine year old, I was deep into the maze of my skewed perceptions and was angry at my parents for not knowing what had happened, yet, more angry at myself for not telling them about the incident. I actually had enjoyed the pleasurable sensations and had not wanted to stop the man, but I didn't know what questions they might ask me, and feared admitting I had allowed it to happen. My mother had always disapproved whenever she had seen me masturbating on my pillow in bed so I sensed that having done something similar with a stranger outside would definitely fall into the disapproval side of the fence. My fear was not because I thought I had done something wrong. I felt powerless to share with them that I sensed something naturally beautiful had happened to me. I felt fractured, splintered by the guilt that I was keeping something significant from my parents yet I did not feel certain or strong enough to share it. I somehow knew that in my little world, I would be judged as inadequate or not being in control, and I protected myself from that. I feared seeming weak or vulnerable, yet I felt strong in knowing that nothing wrong had occurred.

I was angry that I did not trust them to know I was okay with what happened. I did not want any curtailing of my freedom to wander the neighborhood. But I was saddened that their world would see something undesirable with a sensation that I innately knew as innocently pleasurable. Parts of me continued to attend school, play, wander alone all over town on my bike, yet I felt no wholeness, no "me." There was a disconnect. I couldn't feel an inside core. It was not because of the incident with the man, it was because I refused to trust my parents and their world.

I despised the experience of the incident and stopped sensing anything within my heart. I felt a continuous pinpoint in my gut of resentful humiliation. The ignominy seemed mixed with sadness that I had been reluctant to make the man stop, yet with frustration that I was *expected* to make him stop. I had liked it. I continued to pleasure myself without compunction or doubt. But I did feel shadowed for not telling my parents and despondent that they, and everyone else hadn't earned enough trust from me so I *could* tell them. I made people pay for that discrediting feeling of impotence.

Here I was, a clear spirit consciousness barely a decade into experiencing as a human being, and already so expert at savoring the flavors of fear-based illusion. Such power unfolds itself in this mysterious gift of free will. I chose an artificially mind-contrived pain instead of the heart's trustingly childlike joy. I relinquished freedom and hid behind fear.

Reflection: The Child Frolics in the Garden of Innocence

As a child, I did not cognitively apprehend, but I did heart-feel the divine ecstasy within which I and all creation had been eternally birthed. My mind did not understand, but my inner heart-gut knew that as a sensate being, every fiber of my body-mind echoed with the sacred rhythms of the cosmos. I did not yet recognize bodily pleasure as one strand of the divine rapture that encompasses all passionate creativity in the arts and in nature's own flowing pulse. Yet I did know and enjoy arousal. The body I was beginning to identify with seemed to breathe on its own, and my senses told me I was separate from the "other." I did not remember, as grace has now allowed me to, that actually, *I am being breathed by the One, and that I am enfolded within Love's ecstatic embrace.*

There is only Love's vibration. This Source has shared its entirety, its fulsome bliss, **with** itself **as** its God-Self, that is, **as** me and all creation. That sharing is not a division or an apportionment. There are not some people who got "Super-Sized" and others who got a dribble. It is the mystery of Divine Wholeness becoming me. It is divinely infinite potential unfolding itself *as* any and every imaginable choice of any and every creature. That Divine Wholeness is sexuality or the passion of life itself, in its every expression, physical, mental, emotional, and etheric. That Divine Wholeness is abundance in its every potential. Each human is in essence the never-ending flow of abundance and the genderless and innocent ecstasy of sexuality. All creation exists, by its very being, as the Divine Love's self-recognition. Everything in creation then pulses as the creative Self-love and within its frequency of rapturous gratitude.

This truth seems somehow to become obscured in us in our childhood. True spirituality is a remembering and a joyful reclaiming of our God-potential. It is a knowing that the self is not just the body-mind, magnificent as it is, but the pure spirit which utilizes the body-mind as a communication tool when that spirit-consciousness chooses to experience being incarnate. Children in their innocence totally immerse in the present moment, rapturously involved in however that moment captivates them. Then as we humans grow conditioned to others' voices laying down labels, criteria, rules, and limits, a sense of unworthiness develops, and we limit ourselves in such immersion. A feeling of, "too good to be true," begins to seep into the passionate enjoyment of any experience. It is viewed as an indulgence rather that the unquestioning childlike enjoyment of life's passions.

Abundance, another facet of our God-Self, begins to get compartmentalized as we grow out of childhood. Time becomes an issue. Time itself is a fear-based expression of a growing sense of limitation. A child immerses in the momentous enjoyment of the present. As a sense of lack encroaches on our innate knowing of abundance, we tend to fear and horde. Ignoring the abundance of each moment as we breathe it, we conjure up comparisons to past moments or we fret about a scarcity and lack that the future might hold. Freedom and joy spring from being at heart the child each of us is, creating as the God-Self, its own moment-by-moment experiences from the wellspring of our birthright: sexuality and abundance.

There is nothing outside of God. As God-Self, there is nothing outside of me. I, *as everyone and everything*, was loved into existence by the Creator and gifted the power and the responsibility of choosing to experience what I desired. If my immeasurably vast soul elected to experience as a nine-year-old, the illusion of an age-old sadness, a raging, volcano of suppressed anger and resentment, or a hardened resistance to being loved, it could do so. It was only when I began to flow into the unraveling of that identity as body-mind alone, that I began to lessen my need to be guilty.

"Sexuality/Abundance" Human Essence (Sketch by author)

Garden Reverie

In childhood, I knew my and everyone's innocence but could not express it in my child's world. Now, in my seventh decade of life, I once again "… become as the little child," and I, "… enter the kingdom of heaven." (Matthew 18:3) What I am actually doing is entering into a remembrance. I enter into an awareness of the indwelling God-Self. I now begin the return to an awareness of never-lost innocence and awe. I begin to heal in grateful identity with Love. And as I grow in awareness of never-lost innocence and wholeness, I let go my grip on guilt and thus the grip on my "need" to be punished. Yes, I begin to cease creating "punishable" experiences.

I have always celebrated the body, the mind, the spirit, all as God-made and beautifully capable of any experience it desires. As a child, I sensed this. As an adult I recognize it and can verbalize it as the ever-present current of rapture that is my essence. I am the creation of a God ecstatically in love with Itself who shared its fullness *as* me, as the essence of sexuality and abundance. However, a debris field of guilt seems to surround the human psyche in regard to sex. Humans confuse sex and what we deem, "sexual," with our essence *as* sexuality. This springs from our solidly fused identity with the body-mind.

I consider everything sexual, in the broadest sense possible. How could it be otherwise? I am in a bodily form which has senses and organs for receiving and giving heightened awareness of this ecstasy. My essence *is* rhapsody and pulse and my body is the communication tool for this rhythmic bliss, pure and simple. Be it agony or ecstasy, I vibrate with the energy of continuously unfolding potential, and when I stifle or label it, I interfere with its natural flow.

Nothing is unacceptable, even if it flows from what seems to be the basest of motives. God is everything. God is Love. Love does not make mistakes in loving Itself. Humans can synthesize the earthly vibratory delights of God-made colors, sounds, motions, tastes, scents, and textures into a smorgasbord of sense experience and apply it to passionate inspiration *or* to tortured degradation of each other. It is still God in its unfolding gift of non-judged free will. We each dance with each other in what ebbs and flows as history but which is innately the mysterious and divinely funded field of soul-contracts freely chosen and acted out by each of us. We are eternally interchanging our choices to be teacher and student, enlightened sinner and shadowed saint, all within the joyfully innocent, victimless choice points of free will.

I am learning to suspend judgment, of myself or anyone. I recognize that we humans, birthed within the eternal pulsing of Self-Love's ecstatic jubilation, can reverentially utilize our body-minds to generate any experience we desire, until we learn to allow it to flow from Truth and not from perceived victimhood. I am a student of self-mastery, apprenticing myself to the craft of choosing to act from love in every moment. I am learning that I am the human extension of Love in earthly form. In practice, I feel that if I desire to, I can step in and stop or allay others' actions or words which seem to harm or diminish. I can do anything within my power to *be* Love in action. But I do not judge. Everything is neutral. Because of the magnificently prodigal gift of free will, Love in its many forms, arises and passes away as history. Nothing is judged, because God is all there is. I can change the way I look at anything and see only as a child, fearing or loving.

Could not we humans fulfill our trek towards enlightened awareness of Oneness by realizing that it is our attitudes which enable our suffering, and it is our letting go of these perceptions which is our awakening freedom? Can we not do both in the name of a higher good, our very own higher good? It is the at-one-ment, the Atonement, the *knowledge* of Oneness. I, with my sacred and honorable human body, choose to extend the Good, the Holy, and the Beautiful to all with whom I share any moments of earthly encounter.

No matter what religion or form of spirituality I ascribe to, I can communicate from the Christ View. This is not a religious view. It is the view that a fellow named Jesus, or Jeshua in his native Aramaic, arrived at. This is the view that I am the face of God here on earth. I am pure, divinely delighted laughter in human form. Complaining and judgment, in any forms, have no place in my life.

We humans have ripped asunder the fabric of our godly rapture by mentally fusing and bodily identifying as either male or female. We are each, and collectively, in genderless unity of all the aspects of divine masculine and divine feminine. The child knows this innately, not yet having forgotten its heavenly essence. We adults continue to cry out in self-made hell: the male anguish of, "I've got to get this right," to please the partner, or to continue an illusory role of dominance, forgetting his birthright found in the deep joy of surrender. Meanwhile the female stifles her genuine hunger and her knowing power imbedded in receptivity, so she does not appear too "threatening." This is complete denial of our indwelling godliness. Our human bodies are divinely powerful instruments of inherent contentment. At any moment, the glandular system can flood us with well-being, if we joyfully, playfully allow it to. We can go through any day and any night with a bodily and spiritual hard-on. We can let it explode or diffuse at will, through physically sexual interaction with another or with self or through a continuously mindful flow of loving-kindness in gesture, laughter, and daily routine. Allowance and fearless exploration are the keys.

Peace explodes within us when we surrender to this reality and relinquish the body to itself, without the mind's "shoulds" and "shouldn'ts." When we become again as the little child, delighting in the Creator's garden, the Kingdom *will* come. Truly in curiosity, I pose this question, "Could the Second Coming be the Divine Peace that would flood the earth if every man, woman, and child empowered by an innate understanding of sexuality and abundance, released inhibition and in the same orgasmically holy instant of the heart, climaxed together in body, mind, and spirit, experiencing the powerfully beautiful truth of our being?" It could be the passion expressed by the visual artist or the dancer, the committed gardener, the focused athlete, or the spelunker, the inventor, heavy equipment operator, and manicurist. It could be the couple in the throes of sexual embrace, or the threesome or multiplicity of folks in innocent sexual discoveries. Or it could be thrilled children in awe as they splash and play in mud puddles. Consider the surgeon with her poised scalpel, the stand-up comic hearing laughter from an audience, or the proud parents witnessing a child's first steps. Any human endeavor in its culminating moment of deep satisfaction is the instant where each of us, "… is getting it." It does not matter in whichever situation the expression of godliness occurs. It is the very same rooted sexuality and abundance of our Divine Origin which fuels our passions, any passion, and excites our bodies and souls. It is God in human form ecstatically loving Itself and beholding, "It is good." (Genesis 1:31)

How is that for a Second Coming of the Christ View? The Big Bang of human consciousness.

Prayer: *(Adapted from Chapter 5 of the "Way of the Heart," terms)*

Awed Gratitude

Oh, God, I am astonished that you would create me with your same divine ability to

DESIRE.

Just as you desired to share your ineffable power within the gift of free will, I DESIRE to honor you by exercising it freely. May it be only to further Love's Light!

Thank you for the power of Desire!

Oh, God, I am astonished that you would create me with your same divine ability to INTEND.

Just as you intended to make this gift of free will to be infinitely open-ended, I INTEND to honor you by continually discovering new ways I can extend your face of Love within the circle of my daily interactions with all of creation.

Thank you for the power of Intention!

Oh, God, I am astonished that you would create me with your same divine ability to ALLOW.

You unconditionally allowed us humans to explore with no limit your gift of free will. I freely admit that I used this powerful gift to make the impossible seem real. I freely admit that I allowed fear to create "otherness." I now ALLOW your Love to extend AS me, and in reverence for the sovereign right of every being to express itself without my judgment.

Thank you for the power of Allowance!

Oh, God, I am astonished that you would create me with your same divine ability to SURRENDER.

You lovingly surrendered the eternality of creation to whatever we human would do with it, ourselves included. You saw that it was good, because there can be nothing but you. I now SURRENDER to my power to BE you, to be your Love, to be your Light, to be your ever unfolding Joy.

Thank you for the power of Surrender!

Chapter Ten

The Advance to Journeyman in the Art of Illusion

Late Summer 1955 – Bayside, New York (Multiple Days Condensed to One.)

A Busy Adolescent

It's Saturday. The workmen won't be back 'til Monday. This'll be fun.

I dragged the hose over to drench the bags of cement stacked inside the basement of the nearly finished house. In 1955, nobody fenced in home construction sites. I slashed open a dozen bags, shoveled sand over, and mixed it in. It was difficult, but I was strong for a twelve-year-old girl. I opened the spigot completely, and turned the hose onto the mess I'd made. I pictured it being lumpy and hard by Monday. Loving the way the water sprayed out hard, I aimed it at the electrical wiring and the opened fuse box, too, before I strolled out to the street, leaving the hose turned on high.

It was only 10:00 am, by the hourly bells ringing in the church on the corner. I skipped a few blocks to another house under construction, checked that no one was around, and found bulkhead doors unlocked. Feeling my way down to the basement, I spied, in the dim light, a pile of broken up packing crates. Inspired by an almost empty gasoline can next to the generator stored nearby, I dribbled the gasoline onto the wooden stack. I struck a long match on the box of Blue Diamonds I always carried with me, threw it down, and hoped it would burn nice and hot.

*Whoa, that went up fast! Lucky I have white eyebrows. Nobody will notice
I don't have any today. I hope my face isn't blistery.*

I panted heavily with the fright of the near miss to my eyes and the
accumulating black smoke.

Scrambling back up the cellar stairs, I paused at the top and peered
out to make sure nobody had come near. I left the bulkhead doors open,
snuck behind pallets of red bricks out to the sidewalk and skipped down
the block. At the far corner, I sat on the curb and drew tic-tac-toe games
on the asphalt with the chalk I'd pilfered from my sixth grade classroom
in June. I wanted to hang around because I was pretty sure the fire would
die out before it did any real damage. After a while, I ambled in the other
direction and began to skip back towards my own block. I was relieved that
the house would not burn down and happy that I felt that way.

I wasn't hungry enough to go home for lunch yet, so I sauntered over
to the Friedman's house on the corner of my street. I knew they went
away each weekend, so I let myself in through the cellar window I had
left unlocked from previous forays. I liked the Friedman family and it felt
good in their cozy and organized home. I loved exploring their house, and
especially staring at the colorful fish in Mr. Friedman's gigantic tanks. He
had expensive equipment and unusual exotics. I liked the way his angel
fish laid eggs on the sides of the rocks. I only had zebra fish and guppies,
some Amazon swordtails, and a blue gourami in my tanks, but I was proud
of my set up and respected his. I looked forward to someday having egg
layers raising a brood in my tank too.

After exploring the upstairs bedrooms, where I was careful not to
disturb anything, I returned to the basement and left the way I got in.
I lingered in their backyard, landscaped in slate and ivy, and lay on
my stomach hanging over the edge of the goldfish pond, watching the
mosquito larvae hatching out. I made a mental note to return later to net
some larvae for my own fish to eat.

I felt hungry, wondering what I might find in our refrigerator for lunch
if I went home now. I sidled into the narrow alley between the garages,
shimmied up the sturdy maple sapling onto the roof of the Friedman's
garage, and scurried across the shingled rooftop. Hopping from theirs
to the Murphy's garage, I continued upward on the slope, pausing only

to walk along the apex, balancing like a tightrope walker, then edged on down, careful not to step onto the last shingle overhang. I jumped down onto the un-mowed grass and crossed through the Murphy's backyard to ours.

Once there, I spent considerable time teasing my seven-year-old brother on the swing set, calling him *Lukie.* I knew he hated that nickname. I stopped only when Ginny yelled at me. As the oldest of us five kids, she usually got stuck with minding Luke and five-year-old Rita, because I'd leave the house to roam the neighborhood before anyone else was up. I ran into the house to slap together a peanut butter and jelly sandwich and chocolate milk. Mom was busy upstairs with Rosemary, the baby, so I played with our two black cats, Dilly and Daffy, fed them, and crept out the front door before she knew I'd been home. I loved the furtive feeling as I pretended to be in the heroic French resistance fighters I'd heard about recently.

Down the block, in the empty lot next to Basil's house, I grabbed at the rocks hiding the buried foxhole shovel I'd shoplifted at the Army-Navy store. Uncovering the camouflaged entrance to the tunnel I had dug, and lying on my stomach, I excavated a few feet longer and wider into the tunnel. I planned to lure Coretta into the tunnel, so I could bury her. I didn't know how long she would be in it before she got herself out but it sure would scare her. She was only eleven, and I didn't like her being so pretty. I pondered how I might be able to cave it in on her. Hiding the shovel again, I went home to get my bike.

For the next few hours, I explored Crocheron Park, stopping to lie on my back in the grass and watch the clouds. I held my breath as the darning needles landed on me, and I lifted my hand out for the butterflies to land on, too. They liked the sweetness of the bubble gum phlegm I spat in my palm for them. I loved to watch them roll down the proboscis and suck up the spittle.

I rode over the wooden pedestrian bridge spanning Cross Island Parkway and down to Bayside Yacht Club on Little Neck Bay. The tide was low and I clambered on the grungy, blackish rock piles and jetties, collecting the narrow, flesh colored balloons that washed on shore from sewage pumped into the bay. I didn't know why my mother always got upset when I would bring them home, but I liked the way they fit on my fingers and that they were transparent yet strong. They made good mini water balloons. I remembered to pick up some hefty rocks to toss from the bridge down onto the parkway traffic on my way back over.

It was almost dark and I felt hungry again. On my way home, I passed a house with a big picture window. I could see a family sitting together watching television and an aggrieved emptiness welled up in me. I stopped, sneaked nearer, found a big flat rock in their garden, and heaved it through the window. The crash and falling glass frightened me. I hesitated before hopping on my bike to ride home frantically. That must have been how they were able to follow me. I pedaled the few blocks home, pumping furiously the whole way, straight up to our front porch, crashed the bike on the ground and took the stairs two at a time. Slamming through the front door, I scrambled and tripped my way up to the third floor bedroom I shared with Ginny in the attic.

I could hear a car brake in front of our house, the doorbell ring, and then loud voices inside the front door. Modulated conversation ensued. My father, ever the trial lawyer, must have handled the intrusion. I heard Ginny entertaining Luke and Rita in a second floor bedroom. I flopped on my bed, expecting to be summoned at any minute. Crashing rock and the tinkling of broken glass echoed in my brain. I felt terrified, but bored with waiting. Nobody summoned me downstairs. No one, furious or otherwise, came up to get me.

When the car left, I lay face up on my bed, confused and troubled. I felt relieved at the lack of immediate confrontation, but disappointed at yet another unaddressed transgression. I fell asleep, still in my clothes, remorseless, exhausted, and feeling unnoticed. The next day nothing was said; nothing happened. I had a vague sense that money must have passed hands - again. Resentful, I wanted to know what it felt like to be punished, but I feared the disgrace and dismissiveness that I expected would be part of the consequence.

I entered seventh grade a week later at the Catholic parochial school, which I'd attended since first grade. The nuns were strict but I was too cowardly to directly invite their heavy-handed discipline. Instead, my rebellion leaked out in silly acts of whispering, or dropping items on the floor during class. In day dreaming, I undressed the nuns and paraded them around naked in the neighborhood, commanding my own version of Mao's Red Brigade.

At lunch time each day, raging inwardly at myself but wanting to control a perimeter around me, I mercilessly ridiculed my classmate, Meredith, targeting her because of her sweetness. I intimidated Daniel, the class runt, making jokes about his jug-handle ears. During stickball at recess, through sheer bravado and inventive cursing, I enforced, and sometimes concocted the rules, loudly daring anyone to defy my attempts at control. I was a seething cauldron of anger, boiling over onto my pals and classmates, too ashamed of how fragile I felt, too frenetic to slow down and ask for help. Because I saw myself as alone and separate, it never occurred to me to ask for help.

Reflection: I Wonder

What's the root of the energies that seem to fuel my default wiring?

This is a *forgiving* book. It is a book for giving - and living - compassion. The word *compassion* indicates a "sharing of *passion with,*" that is, a *willingness to allow* and be strong in the bearing of your own and your neighbor's unfolding potential of expression. It is the unfolding of the God-Self's right to deeply, authentically, feel its chosen vibratory energies in human form.

The book's vignettes illustrate how quickly and easily, as a baby, young child, and then teen-ager, I spent years constructing the illusion of "them and me." Fear is an inevitable part of the illusion of separation. Perhaps it is the thoroughness of my identity as body-mind which rooted these vibrations as my default wiring. And this was the energetic wiring that ran my experience-making throughout my life. Underneath a veneer of "knowing everything," I hid a smoldering fear of appearing inadequate to whatever task lay before me and/or of being uncovered as a phony. I was looking outside myself for approval and affirmation instead of finding it deep within me. I utterly refused to admit to mistakes or lack of ability. This shaky approach to life demanded constant mental maneuvering and an anxiety-riddled lack of truthfulness.

With advanced age came a bit of wisdom. When I had dug to the facts of my birth dynamics and seen that the timing and placement of my birth choices had placed me smack dab into a *"Pleeeeeze, Mommy! Pick me up! Pick me up! ... Please, just notice me,"* psyche and framework of reference, I began to show myself compassion. I began to laugh even at the joke I had played on myself, just as all we humans do. I had taken my fears seriously. I had taken the game of illusion seriously. Grace, which is the Inner Comforter, has opened me to an awareness that I can make a moment-by-moment choice to remember and claim the inherent power of happiness. I can once again grow aware of a never-broken, but unremembered connection to Source. Stepping into this joyful inheritance, I breathe gently and deeply, and ground my immeasurable spirit and divine expansiveness into my physical body. With a slow, full breath, I call back any part of my soul that I have scattered in fearful, shadowed forgetfulness that I am unconditionally loved. With slowed, deeper breathing comes awareness of the Truth of my divinity. With this remembering comes the recognition of a Sonship with innate and total invitation to explore every possible vagary of life's potential. This illuminates me. I become aware of all us beings, healing into a claimed wholeness born of a conscious awareness of having once stepped into a dream-world of identity with guilt. I willingly step out of this dream-world and rejoice in the child's inherent innocence. Heaven and earth are united. I have become, "... as the little child," who will, "... enter the kingdom." The Kingdom/Queendom is celebrated as being within, and as, Self.

Segment II

1961 - 1970

Human Forgetfulness Fuses to Identity
The Journeyman Chooses the Illusion of
Unworthiness as Her Specialty

Chapter Eleven

The Journeyman Flaunts Her Skills Extending the Illusion of Suffering

None-Sense

In my family's home in the 40's and 50's, I learned geography and an appreciation of other cultures through two magazines. One was published by the National Geographic Society and the other by the Maryknoll missionary men and women. The pictures in National Geographic inspired the naturalist in me, but the exploits of the Maryknoll missionaries fed my soul and my adventuresome spirit.

In senior year of high school I had covertly been communicating with the Maryknoll Sisters in upstate New York to enter their novitiate to become a missionary nun. This was by no means inspired by religious feelings, but rather by a yearning for foreign adventure. I wanted to live among indigenous peoples, share their language, and assist them in bettering their future. I was not aware of the news surrounding the formation of Peace Corps efforts, nor of other church-run charities. As a product of Catholic school for twelve years, becoming a missionary nun seemed my only option for adventure. True to the assumed energy of guarded self protection, I kept my interests and communication with Maryknoll a secret from my parents lest they somehow show disapproval. I wanted it to be a *fait accompli* before I told them.

I had not shared my aspirations with my family, and was dimly aware that my parents had never questioned me about my plans after graduation. But, by choice, I was around them very little at that time. I left for school before they were up, and if not staying over a friend's house, or serving detention after school for numerous disciplinary infractions, or playing in interschool basketball, I returned home late, after catching a subway and two city buses. Usually secretive about my plans anyway, I feared interference or even well-intentioned advice. But my parents' subscription to Maryknoll Magazine certainly was instrumental in shaping the course of my life's journey.

I seemed to be two people at once, because at home I made myself hard to love, but at school was quite gregarious and popular. I had outgrown my adolescent efforts at angry vandalism. My classmates had nominated me for student government offices in each undergraduate year, and I was by then president of the Student Association. This was much to the consternation of the nuns because for four years I had spent my daily classroom efforts breaking rules and causing disciplinary havoc. It was quite an easy feat, actually, given that most Catholic high schools up through the 50's were replete with obsolete rules, inspired by medieval attitudes toward the role of women. I was fortunate to have received a classically grounded, Jesuit-based education, but it was sternly enforced by officiously righteous nuns, and I found delight in undermining their humorless exertions.

A casual question however, from Sister Rose Maria, the Prefect of Discipline, changed the focus of my plans and "the first shoe dropped." I was in her office, serving a double detention for playing hooky the day before and not wearing my white gloves at the Friday whole-school assembly. She mentioned that she had not seen my choice for colleges posted in the notices. When I tentatively shared my Maryknoll intentions with her, she blasted me with a red-faced, "But *we* have missions too, you know!" My fate was sealed.

Confounded at having been "outed," I never once resisted. I went along with her insistence on being my "sponsor" to enter the novitiate of their teaching order in mid Long Island. Once again, the groveling need for approval and love reared its head. Classroom teaching was the furthest thing from my mind, but when a free college education for me was presented to my parents, I found myself uncharacteristically compliant. However, something was definitely awry. The summer after high school graduation, I would habitually wake at two or three in the morning and aimlessly drive the family car eastward from our home in Douglaston. I would find myself on the highway near Jones Beach, not remembering how I had gotten there. Anxiety was quite rooted. I was sharpening my skills in an apprenticeship in victimhood.

Inexorably, time marched on. July ended, and close family members gathered at our house to wave a fond farewell. My immediate family piled into our two-tone green 1956 Dodge station wagon with myself at the wheel, for supposedly the last time I would ever drive a car. Fifty miles to the east, a large group of us innocently trusting new hopefuls dutifully clad in black, gathered in the novitiate that sweltering day. We were surrounded by family and friends sending us off into a world of veils, vows, and mystery. Most of the families seemed reluctant to let go, fearing for their daughters' entering a world shrouded in the blessed, but unknown. I suppose the families were hoping we had each made a sound decision. Finally, urged by Sister Agnella, our Mistress of Postulants, the well-wishers tearfully bade farewell and drove off.

Now we were officially postulants in the Congregation of the Sisters of St. Philip, dressed entirely in black calf-length skirts, black lisle stockings and sturdy, laced pumps. We had long sleeved black blouses, capes, and short black veils with a white cuff allowing a crop of hair to show at the top and sides of our heads. We were sixty young women, most of us eighteen or nineteen years of age. A few who were in their late twenties, seemed venerable to the rest of us for having been out in the working world and thus making a decision based more on experience than the seeking of approval or humble servitude.

We were swept up in the culmination of dreams and reveries, some life-long, some, like mine, based on the shaky sands of doubt or disinclination. But mystery beckoned, service sang a siren song, and we followed, determined to make the best of it. This wasn't the Maryknoll order, and I wasn't being prepared for faraway missions, but it was the unknown, an adventure nonetheless, and I threw myself into the life with a zealous, determined effort to excel.

In 1961, the convent grounds were a sprawling complex. The motherhouse itself was an enormous yellow brick building, annexed on either side by a church of cathedral proportions, and a novitiate with dorms, classrooms, library, and common rooms. It was situated in the middle of its own apple orchards, strawberry fields, a nuns' cemetery, and a working dairy farm. It was all part of the motherhouse acreage situated in the still-rural mid Long Island countryside. Separate buildings on the vast grounds of the order's motherhouse served as a boarding school for girls from kindergarten through high school. There were stables and an exercise ring for the girls' horses. A newer structure to one side was a secondary novitiate specifically for those further along in the process of dedication and college courses. Then there were the single-use houses for maintenance workers and visiting priests. A nuns' retirement home and a pool area would be added during my five years spent (or misspent, depending on one's perspective) in this expansive countryside pocket of dedication.

As soon as our families left, we were placed in groups of six and introduced to our "Angels." These were select second-year novices, two years our senior in the novitiate process, who would each be responsible for shepherding their half dozen shell-shocked charges through the first few months of adjustment.

We were then paraded outside to the sheds where the last of the corn harvest awaited our inexpert but very willing processing. This proved the first of countless moments of apprehension and self recrimination, as a dour, overbearing little old nun harassed us on our inefficient "shucking" of the corn. In fact, we were forlorn, nervous wrecks, and this certainly, in our young minds, was akin to boot camp slave labor. I tried desperately, but to no avail, to win the slave driver's blessing of my technique and growing pile of shucked and "silkless" ears of corn. I soon slid back into my high school mode of deliberately exasperating the woman. It didn't take long for my old pattern of deceptive surreptitious sabotage to rear its ugly head.

When I entered that order of nuns in 1961, the novitiate process until final vows were taken was originally three years. Eventually, the novitiate included a four year teaching college accredited by the New York State Department of Education. However that four years was punctuated by a full academic year where no "secular" subjects were studied. Instead we concentrated on accredited courses in comparative religions, New Testament and Old Testament biblical studies, Gregorian chant and church music, Christology, and theology, philosophy, morals, and ethics. This extended the college career to a five year stint when we finally graduated and were awarded our New York State teaching certification, Grades K – 6.

I was actually a bundle of contradiction, at war within myself. Desperate for the approval of the nuns in charge of us, I went over and above in compliance with the rules when I could be observed. But whenever I could I resentfully looked for shortcuts to chores, and sought out secretive ways to explore the labyrinthine passageways of the Motherhouse building and the connecting hallways of the novitiate and dorms. As postulants and novices, we worked long sweaty hours in the steam-filled laundry rooms, the noisy, spray-filled dishwashing area in the refectory, or the endless cleaning and polishing of the dorms, hallways, and meeting rooms of the buildings.

Sister Paul Marie with grandparents in front of novitiate.

For the ensuing five years within the novitiate and the following four years of classroom teaching, compliance with the vows of chastity, poverty, and obedience never fazed me: I just ignored them. I was enthralled by the feminine energy oozing from an establishment reigned over and supervised by women. For me there seemed an overriding eroticism within convent walls that fed my comfortably bisexual nature and allowed me to bury my depression and anxious defensiveness. Because these energies seemed rooted in a career where I was commanded to be an English teacher instead of an adventurer and scientist, my acquiescence masked an underlying discontent. Unconscious then, of what I know now, I blamed Sister Rose Maria and most of the professors at the teaching college, for what I perceived as forcing me into something that seemed 180° from what I had wanted to do with my life. I blamed my parents for what I perceived as not building up my trust in them enough so that I could admit to them that I had made a mistake in joining that order of teaching nuns. The shit hit the fan though, when my "blame game" targeted innocent children entrusted to my care.

Autumn 1966 – Long Island, New York

Loathing Self in Another

The seven-year-old huddled against the swirling wind, her entire body visibly trembling in the corner of the school yard. She pulled a shabby thin sweater tightly around her frail body but it did nothing to shield her bare legs exposed to the biting October wind. She wore no hat and with just a white hair bow clipped into thin, barely combed hair it was hard not to surmise *family difficulties*. This little girl needed nurturing. Her eleven-year-old sister seemed to be crumpling under the burden of an assumed mothering role. She needed an advocate, too.

I was the nun on duty in the school yard that crisp morning. Even through the thick black wool serge of my habit I could feel the vicious tug of the wind. For protection, I pulled the woolen shawl more tightly around my shoulders. My mind and body registered that forlorn little girl's discomfort, but my heart remained as icy as the chilly wind. I waited impatiently for the bell to ring, pacing in agitation, not so much to end the child's pain but as a relief to the edginess I felt about it.

Her aloneness and sense of resignation stirred in me a dim memory of shabby clothing. I was annoyed that her parents sent her to school that way but I would not move myself to help her. I did not wrap my warm, extensive shawl around her or even just move nearer her so that my billowing woolen skirt could block her from the freezing gusts. I stood inert, not willing to step into something I sensed would get complicated, if I began to protect her. I pretended I didn't see her.

The little one's older sister was in my sixth grade. She came into the classroom each morning, scrambling to finish homework before the first period began. She didn't seem to socialize. During the parent-teacher conference in September, her father had come by himself. He confided that although their mother was there at home, he tried his best to be both parents. With an empathetic look pasted on my face, I stayed uninvolved, refusing to be emotionally entangled. I was struggling with self doubt and confusion about my own life, and felt too fragile to shoulder someone else's burdens. In a self-absorbed, "poor me" attitude, I refused to take any initiative to help him.

When the older sister began to fail my quizzes and tests, I did not offer to tutor her after school. Whenever I sensed her gaze upon me, a queasy, unsettling heaviness seemed to ooze upward from the soles of my feet and into my legs. It streamed into my torso, my innards. As she eyed me, I saw myself, in that same sense of being on the outside of life, looking in. The feeling sent shivers of self-loathing through me which I turned upon her in thinly disguised disdain. As her grades spiraled downwards, so did my own self-esteem. I told myself she'd just have to face the consequences. I did not want to look at the "us." When she failed the final exam, I didn't pass her to the next grade.

These two girls reminded me of myself. In my own frailty and fractured view, I felt I had failed us all.

Spring 1967 – Brooklyn, New York

Hangin' Rope

Lucy, don't open this door. Don't open it, Luce. Don't, don't, don't . . .

My brain raced, partly terrified of confrontation, but equally and hysterically amused at the silliness of the situation. I crouched in Sister Lucy's darkened closet, where I had jumped when Sister Gertrudis, suddenly pounded on Lucy's bedroom door that spring afternoon. As the Mother Superior here at our local convent, she was demanding that I come out of the room. I perched on a pile of Lucy's shoes, knowing that Sister Gert could easily reach out from the opened bedroom doorway where she stood, and slide the closet door open. I tried to stifle a giggle as I pictured myself tumbling out at her feet. Lucy, constant under fire, claimed she didn't know what Gertrudis was talking about. She refused to slide open the closet door and asked Gertie to leave.

Lucy's bedroom was two doors down the hall from mine. It wasn't easy to avoid detection as I crept down there each night to share her bed. We had been a couple since Thanksgiving Day the previous year, when on a walk together, I admitted that I was in love with her. I was twenty four years old, on my first convent assignment, to teach sixth grade. I had arrived with a darkened reputation earned from my rebellious editorials in our novitiate's college newspaper, where I had supported the Jesuits' Berrigan brothers in their anti-war escapades. She was seventeen years my senior and admired my moxie. We had started with long walks together, but our affair swiftly moved to her bedroom and my overnight stays.

This was in the afternoon though, and we had just been hanging out in her room, fully clothed and laughing about an amusing incident in her classroom that day. We had been inseparable during all those months and were sloppy about covering our tracks, encouraged by the presence of another couple within the group of sixteen nuns in this convent. The Mother Superior probably saw it as epidemic proportions.

Close to apoplexy now, Sister Gertrudis croaked,

"I've spoken to Monsignor McElroy about this situation and he said to give you two enough rope and you'd hang yourselves."

She added, "I know you're in there now, Sister Paul Marie. And I know you sneak down here every night. I'm giving you fair warning."

She stalked away, and I waited until dinner to come out of Lucy's room.

Sister Lucy and I didn't meet in her room any more. Instead, we went to her father's place in Greenpoint on weekends. The vow of chastity didn't stand a chance. There was a reason we were admonished in the novitiate to always hang around in groups of three or more. The convent can be an erotic place.

That summer the motherhouse did its best to separate Lucy and me. She remained in Brooklyn, as the powers-that-be reassigned me further east to a parish school in Nassau County. It became harder to arrange meetings and eventually we gave up. When I told Lucy I finally wanted to face the truth that I didn't belong in convent life and would request a release from my vows, I begged her to leave too, and come to live with me. She said she had already been a nun for twenty four years and was very happy with her life. I felt mine was one big lie.

In late August, I moved to the new parish, after a summer spent toiling in the kitchen and dining rooms of the religious order's summer place in the Hamptons. Two more years passed, filled with confusion and chaos for me, and consequently, cowardly acts of cruel indifference towards the adolescents under my care. I had made quite a mess of my life so far, and the pain spilled over into the lives of the innocents in my care.

Spring 1968-69 - Nassau County, Long Island, NY

Steel Rules

I know I should stop doing this.

I could tell by the eighth graders' faces that this was too much. I'd taken it too far this time. The boy's body had gone rigid, his lanky adolescent frame bent over the side of my teacher's desk in front of the room. His torso lay flat on the desk, making his rear end a helpless, green-corduroy target of my steel ruler wrath. He groaned and gasped with each blow. I knew I was beet red because I sweated in my black wool habit. I could see my knuckles white against my hands as I slammed the flat ruler against him yet another time. The bronze crucifix hanging from the long rosary around my waist clanged against the desk. But I still didn't quit.

You've really gone too far. Stop it!

But I didn't stop. His feet were off the floor, knees bent against the desk, bracing himself. I still didn't stop. I was exhausted with the effort of the measured words I uttered with each forceful thud, "You … will … keep … your … mouth … SHUT." I stopped with that final emphatic outburst, but his body just lay there.

The room was deathly silent, the kids horrified. He slowly let his feet down but he didn't get up.

What's wrong with me?

I felt embarrassed to have lost it, yet my voice quavered with spent rage as I warned, "This young man tested my patience once too many times. I hope you all learned not to push me."

It's all in the control. They can't take advantage if you're in control.

He painfully unbent himself, tried to straighten but could not at first. Shuffling to his desk at the back corner of the room, he stood, straight but pale, waiting for the bell to end the last period of the day. At least I didn't make him sit down this time. I knew he would not tell his father that he'd been in trouble. I felt embarrassed though, that some of the other kids might tell theirs.

*Let **them** try to control 47 teenagers at the end of the day!*
I would not admit to myself that my own life was in shambles. I was sad, confused, and resentful of my own seeming lack of character. The inner maelstrom resulted in unplanned lessons and slack disciplinary skills, which naturally segued into teenagers taking sly advantage of lengthy pauses between my "lesson segments." Thus I resorted to the steel ruler outbursts. I refused to look inside for the cause of my fear and blamed my unhappiness on those outside me. The bell rang and they all filed out quickly, silently, to their good Catholic homes. I walked across the street to my good Catholic convent. We were all sickened, scared, and scarred.

The next day I asked the Mother Superior to write to the bishop requesting that I be released from my vows. Instead of that option, I was offered a post to one of our schools in Puerto Rico. The institution in which I was a rotting apple, did not resist the opportunity to squeeze more juice from me ... to the potential endangerment of yet more trusting children. And I, caroming off yet another wall in my pinball approach to life, avoided the real challenge to my unhappiness and did not resist the opportunity finally, to go to the "missions."

Reflection: Remorse and Forgiveness

That boy was a big kid, jolly and talkative. Actually, he reminded me of myself in the eighth grade, always with a quip, and just going along for the ride. I sensed back then, that when he left my classroom he still had to dodge meanness and indignity. I compounded whatever fear and confusion he felt. But I was not heeding any dim voice of conscience back then. Though I could have shown him how lovable he was, I debased him even more. Instead of allowing him to discover and trust his own abilities, I robbed him of his sense of worth. I humiliated and blamed him. I turned around and wrought upon this child and scores of other children the demeaning, control-based discipline that was the only system I knew from my own twelve years of Catholic school education. I continued the spiral of fear-based control to hide my deep confusion and pain.

I am not suggesting an excuse for the misery I caused during certain periods of my life. The majority of Catholic school survivors went on to lead lives filled with purposeful compassion and productive empathy. The falsely perceived frailty and inadequacy at my core informed the wellspring of my harshness. I judged from a self-righteous arrogance and controlled from a base of fear. In denial of my innate beauty and a strength which springs from Truth, I layered everything with a self-loathing which I then projected onto others instead of onto myself.

Mysteriously, the actual source of this fractured outlook, this lack of self love was the power of free will, this gift of God-potential itself. As conscious spirit, I had selected to explore certain vibratory energies. As the coalesced density of a human form, I had played with these energies, identified with them and perceived through them. In being run by them I had achieved a false mastery of them and had not yet begun to listen to my Inner Comforter. I still hid behind an image of piety as I dished out cruelty, woefully unaware of the indwelling Holy Spirit, the essence of my existence. Immersed in my own "victim" attitude, I generated my drama and inflicted pain on another.

To all students who have endured the harshness of Catholic schools, whether you are physically among us or have passed, I apologize for all of us teachers. It will not restore the dignity I stole from you. Would it help you to know my sorrow now and my acknowledgement of your strength and beauty back then? Would you forgive me if you saw that I have forgiven myself my false perceptions of self and my judgment of you? That it was only when I recognized us each and all in our essential innocence and Light-filled beauty, that I could love us each and all? Perhaps it was my jealousy of your wholesome joy, of your innocence. Maybe it was a recognition of something within you that mirrored my own splintered self. Whichever of these, it spurred me to target you or to ignore your plight.

I was the perpetrator of violence this time around. I own it. I chose to be traumatized that way and then turned around and continued the spiral of fear and pain. Sovereign beings of choice, we danced together in the unfolding of free will. Our souls played within the matrix of being both student and teacher. I own my fear-based acts of cruelty and neglect. I ask your forgiveness for having trampled your beauty beneath my pain. I am now learning to forgive myself for not seeing my own beauty or yours back then and for missing the opportunity to share it in mutual joy.

Segment III

1970 – 1983

Human Forgetfulness Entrenched:
Mastery of Victimhood Achieved

Chapter Twelve

The Master of Illusion Spreads her Wings

August 1970 - Puerto Rico

There Are No Coincidences

My first weekend in Puerto Rico, 27 years-old, and wearing the white habit of our mission garb, I drove over the mountain ranges of the island from San Juan on the north coast to Ponce, on the south. The year before, in 1969, in response to the "Agiornamento," or "Open Window" policy of Pope John XXIII, updating the Roman Catholic Church, we voluntarily left behind us the religious names given us by the order. I became Sister Nan Burke instead of Sister Paul Marie. Most of us also changed our cumbersome, medieval widows' garb, for black dresses or calf-length skirts, blouses, and jackets. We wore a modified shorter veil allowing some hair to show above the forehead and on the sides of our heads. For my new venture in the subtropics, I wore a white or grey version of this outfit, with white pumps.

Sister Nan awaiting flight to San Juan, Puerto Rico

My dad gave me cash to rent a car and visit my pal, Gabriela. We remained close friends from the five years we spent in the novitiate college on Long Island. Because we were placed chronologically in every activity and my birthday was May 10th and hers June 14th, we spent the entire five years next to each other at the refectory tables, the chapel pews, the classroom desks in college, the dorms, and the work assignments. Fortunately, we clicked that first day and remained bosom buddies.

She was from Puerto Rico, and along with her twin sister, was raised by her grandfather when her father remarried and grew distant. Her "Abuelo" couldn't visit often from Puerto Rico, so Gabriela joined my family when they visited me on the novitiate grounds. My family became quite fond of her. "Gabi" was assigned to San Ignacio convent in Ponce, during the years I floundered in New York parishes. We hadn't seen each other in the intervening four years and were chomping at the bit to catch up.

I came to Puerto Rico for my new mission, Santa Rosa parish, in Old San Juan, and two days later, drove the four hours across the mountains to the coastal town of Ponce. I intended to pick up Gabriela, and continue west to visit a mutual friend in the old mountain town of San Germán. Little did we know how significant this jaunt would be and how similar our paths would remain, in entirely unexpected ways.

When Gabriela opened the door of her convent that day, it seemed a double-edged sword. We fell into each other's arms, hugging for dear life, but it was much more than innocent nostalgia from novitiate days. From those five years of close, daily sharing, we knew each other's signals. We both could tell that the other had experienced major upheavals, building from a chafing, restrictive, uneasiness in the past year to an impatient, frustrated yearning. Neither of us was willing until now to face that reality.

During our trip, Gabi confided to me that she could not sleep or concentrate because of intense inner turmoil. She had wanted to leave the convent for months, and now found herself embroiled in a mutual attraction with one of the stateside priests in her parish. She seemed relieved to hear of my own struggles with wanting to leave, and chuckled when I shared my involvement with a priest from the Nassau County parish. I never told her about my affair with Sister Lucy.

Father Leo and I had been dating since Lucy had spurned my invitation to build a life together. I did share that after two years of agonizing, I finally admitted to myself I was living a lie and had requested of my superiors to be released from my vows. Leo also, was fast approaching the point of being secularized. It would free him up for a more golf, he'd joked. But I knew he loved the priestly ministry and was thus grieving over the issue of celibacy. We had never consummated our mutual lust, but came close. (Pun intended.) At my request to be relieved of my vows, the motherhouse said that in response to the Vatican Council, they were establishing a less restrictive Mother Superior-less convent in Puerto Rico. If I would rethink my decision, they'd let me try that approach and assign me to the parish of Santa Rosa.

So here I was, months later ready to embark on a new adventure and reuniting with my novitiate pal, Gabriela, in her sub-tropical birthplace. We traveled west along the coast from Ponce, and before turning northward into the mountains, we fatefully stopped for lunch at a tourist spot in La Parguera, the site of a phosphorescent bay.

We saw a color centerfold from that Sunday's edition of *The San Juan Star* on the lobby bulletin board. It featured the hotel's boating facilities, and had underwater photographs of the sea life in the bay fronting the hotel. The article mentioned that one of the divers worked at a new aquarium being built in Isla Verde, east of San Juan. I perked up at that because I intended to learn SCUBA so I could begin to collect my own salt water tropicals for tanks I wanted to build. I noted the location of the future aquarium up north near me, and we ate and left for San Germán. The rest of the trip was filled with the old world charm of colonial style Puerto Rican architecture, mountain coffee plantations, and pineapples in the fertile valley of Lajas.

Gabriela and I poured our hearts out to each other and the seeds of decisions were strewn on the winds. After the trip, I drove back north to San Juan sensing that neither of us would last the year as nuns.

October 1970 – San Juan, PR

Clueless in San Juan

On October 12th, the first school holiday, I signed out the convent car, and drove myself the few miles to the site of the new aquarium in San Juan. It was just east of the airport, on a cliff side overlooking the ocean. I subsequently found out that a Dutch fellow named Han was in the midst of negotiating with the Puerto Rican government for the rights to build and run an aquarium on this former WW II gun battery defense. It seemed vaguely ironic to me that the tides of time would turn wartime anxiety into a peaceful pursuit of educational entertainment. On this day, though, only excavated tunnels and mounds of dirt were evident. The site still had remnants of the rampart of anti-aircraft gun mounts, and I wondered how they would meet the scheduled opening day announced in the newspaper article.

I saw no one when I drove up the cliff side road, so I parked the car, and, trying not to get my white shoes and habit dirty from the swirling, sandy grime, I trudged over to the fence where two workmen appeared from behind a mound. Proud to use my high school and college Spanish, I asked for the *jefe* (boss). They snickered between them, repeating the word, "jefe," and answered that the real jefe wasn't here, but they'd call someone who might help me. After much shouting and echoing at the mouth of one tunnel, there emerged a disheveled, grimy Americano, handsome in a blond, unshaven, grizzled way, unkempt in filthy clothes. He introduced himself with gusto as "Albert Slaughter, as in *kill*." He continued the opening salvo with, "My middle name is Emerson, and I don't know what m'daddy was thinkin' givin' me a Yankee poet's name," and sauntered over to open the gate for me to come inside the construction site. I told him I wanted to learn SCUBA diving to catch marine specimens for my tanks in the convent. He responded enthusiastically that he had planned SCUBA classes for the next two weekends for high school boys in Rio Piedras and that I could join in for free.

For the next two hours, he vigorously led me on a tour of the huge, empty, underground glass tanks fitted into the cavernous holes and huge tunnels around the site. He passionately and meticulously outlined the process of collecting the corals and rocks for building the displays inside each tank. He explained the machinery installed for the filling, aerating, and filtering of the water. Eventually, the diving crew would scour the waters off Puerto Rico to collect sharks, skates, and fish for the larger tanks, and lobsters, shrimp, seahorses, and smaller fish for the tanks along the passageways. Such proximity to this real life technology enthralled me. Traipsing among the mounds of corals being readied for the tanks, and touching the actual machinery already installed, I pictured myself someday swimming among the creatures in the tanks. I totally lost track of time. Albert spread a clean tarpaulin and we sat near the mounds of dirt for another few hours, chatting about our own lives.

The workmen were long gone as Albert, now "Al" to me, regaled me with humorous tales of his Southern Baptist upbringing. He was seventeen years older than I, curiously, the same age as my convent love, Sister Lucy. Born in Roanoke Rapids, North Carolina, the third of eight children, he finished seventh grade when his father took him out of school to work and bring home money during the Depression. His current wife, a Dominican woman, was his fourth attempt at marital bliss. The second and third were the same Puerto Rican woman who divorced, then remarried him, only to divorce him again. An alarm bell ding-donged weakly at this tidbit of info, but I quickly dismissed it.

"The Four Artifacts." (Painting of Albert by author's mother, Virginia K. Burke) (Private collection)

He had four grown children, from his first wife, a woman from the state of California, whom he'd met shortly after he was discharged from the Navy at the end of WW II. The kids came in rapid succession. At present there were two sons, with two children each, and one daughter, not yet married, all living in the state of Oregon. Another daughter lived in Virginia, with her two children, giving Al a total of six grandchildren, none of whom he'd met. Another alarm tinkled here, but even more distantly than the first, and I again cavalierly dismissed it.

He'd joined the Navy at seventeen, with the permission of his parents. Trained as a hard-hat deep sea diver, he served in the Pacific arena during WW II, working à la Jules Verne, in canvas suit, lead weighted boots, and metal helmet. He said that ten years before, he had left a successful SCUBA diving business in the North Carolina area to reside in Puerto Rico. I never asked why he'd do that so precipitately. Another clue was ignored, as once again alarm bells continued sounding, and I shoved them to a remote corner of my brain. Basking in the oddness of it all, I ignored the irony that I had left home at eighteen to walk in the footsteps of a fellow who had told his followers he would make them "fishermen of souls," and that here I was, gulping at Albert's bait and swallowing it all, hook, line, and sinker.

When Al showed me the future shark tank, deep memories of wanting to be a marine biologist stirred in me. My heroine, Dr. Eugenie Clark, like me, was born in New York City and had been interested in fish and marine life since her childhood. She was especially famous for her studies of sharks in the Red Sea. As a child, I dreamed of going on diving expeditions and research voyages like hers. In the novitiate and teaching college, I requested training as a science teacher but the dean told me to major in English because they needed English teachers at the time. Now, in this unlikely, self-described recovering alcoholic, with a North Carolina twang and a sense of humor and penchant for puns, I had found my own Jacques Cousteau. I pictured myself as a Eugenie sidekick. I was smitten by his aura of bravado, his marine exploits, and especially his sense of derring-do. The golf playing ex-priest-to-be rapidly faded to the past, and I half-knowingly embarked on a twelve year odyssey of perilous escapades filled with laughter and heartbreak.

The Rabbit Hole Is Beneath the Palm Tree?

For the next two months, Albert frequently showed up at the convent gates, in the early morning on his way to work, or when homeward bound. The convent and school sat on a busy street, two blocks from the beach, in a residential area, with small apartments for tourists sprinkled among the private homes. Each property had exotic palms and tropical plants, with flowers splayed against the whitewashed or tan plastered houses.

They were walled in or fenced with *rejas* (fancy wrought iron gates and barred windows.) Instead of ringing the bell, Albert would rattle the iron gates loudly and repeatedly yoo-hoo for, "Sister Nan." One of the nuns would seek me out in exasperation, snapping, "That Slaughter fellow is here *again* for you." I chuckled at how he deliberately trifled with them in their righteousness and earnest propriety.

He did follow through on the promise of SCUBA lessons. I continued into the second weekend lesson despite nearly dying from carbon monoxide poisoning the first Sunday. After ten minutes in the pool with the tank on, I developed a splitting headache and searing pain in my chest. I vomited all over the pool deck, then drove home to the convent, bleary-eyed, flopped into bed, and slept through the night. It turned out he'd filled the SCUBA tanks with air drawn in from a gas station garage where the mechanic was running a car motor, doing repairs. Luckily, I didn't pass out during the night, from the carbon monoxide poisoning. Those same dim alarm bells clanged a bit louder as I conveniently ignored the clues and plowed ahead, recklessly sniffing out adventure.

Al certified me after a dive below thirty-three feet from a Boston whaler moored in front of the Hotel San Juan. Through the month of November, we spent every weekend alone, snorkeling and SCUBA diving on the reefs close to shore in Isla Verde. I was in my heaven of sorts, daring to live out my dream, but ignoring my classroom preparation and spiritual life. The five other nuns never questioned me directly, but they seemed perturbed by my unexplained absences and Al's increased presence.

A Tropical Reef in the Maze Too?

One memorable Saturday, we drove in his yellow Volkswagen Beetle, along the packed-sand beach road eastward from the aquarium site. We continued through Los Piñones, towards Loiza, a village settled by black descendants of escaped slaves from the British-held Caribbean islands. When we came to the mouth of the Loiza River, Al whistled to a skinny, grizzled old black man waiting on the other side on his bamboo raft ferry. The man poled his ferry towards us, across the span of the river with the help of a teenage boy wielding a second long pole. They guided the raft, attached alongside a rope-and-post contraption which straddled the length of the crossing. When the raft reached our side of the river, the boy jumped off, pushed it as far up the sandy bank as he could, and threw down two rickety planks. Albert drove the Beetle up onto the raft, I hopped on, the planks were hoisted on board, and off we went, back across the river, poled by the old man and teenager, á la *African Queen*.

We continued a few more miles down the desolate beach, Albert loudly reciting verse upon verse of Robert W. Service's "Spell of the Yukon" poems. It seemed utterly incongruous yet comfortably quirky to me, that we had the subtropical Atlantic on our left, and tall, gangly, windswept palms and beach grass on our right, and here's Albert spewing out ditties about frozen Alaskan tundra. I thoroughly jived on it.

Finally a few wooden shacks appeared, clothes hanging out to dry in the dirt yards, and skinny mutts barking at our passing. After a few more groups of huts, Al stopped the car at one shack, its peeling turquoise paint and tin roof baking in the open air and broiling sun. He shouted a lengthy salutation in Spanish, and an older black couple shuffled out, hoarsely but effusively greeting him with toothless grins and open arms. After much hugging and back slapping, Al turned and introduced me to them as a *monja* (nun.) Their eyes widened in shocked surprise, understandably, since I had rigged up a diving outfit of cutoff jeans and halter top, and wore nothing else except a baseball cap on my curly blonde hair and flip-flops on my feet. They recovered quickly, and greeted me with the same affection.

After we all downed copious amounts of their homemade *limonada*, fresh squeezed from the small brave lemon trees in the yard, Al announced we would leave the car in their patio and begin our snorkeling out in front. I saw nothing but open ocean and in disbelief asked where we'd find fish to spear or lobsters to snare. He pointed far off, out to a line of crashing surf about half a mile offshore, and said we'd snorkel to it. Supposedly, the water was only seven feet deep out there, with plenty of crevices and caves where the groupers, moray eels, and lobsters hung out.

I tried to cover my trepidation with an aloof bravado, but my involuntary shivering unmasked it. I hoped we were far enough away from the mouth of the river because I knew that sharks like to hang out near the outflow of brackish water with whatever garbage and carcasses might float out in the current. The sirens of alarm were now blatantly and distinctly blaring. This time, it was difficult to shove them aside.

"Spell of the Yukon in the Caribbean" cartoon. (Sketch by author)

We donned gardening gloves to protect against the painful sting of sea urchin needles from the reef, and the antennae and fins of the lobsters and fish. We each carried a lobster snare which was simply a length of stiff wire doubled through a short, narrow PVC tube. This formed a loop at one end for slipping around the lobster's curled tail as it rested backed into a cave. I shoved the tubed part into the waistband of my jean cutoffs. Al handed me a spear gun and a net bag with nearly fifty feet of line attached to it. When I asked in Spanish, why so much rope, he laughingly answered that the slack was protection in case a shark decided to snap up our prizes. "That way, they'll leave *you* intact," he chuckled. I figured he was joking, as usual, until I saw the old lady crossing herself as she watched us enter the surf.

We snorkeled the distance to the reef, sometimes over sea grass strewn with conch and sea cucumbers, but most of the time over a wavy, sandy bottom about twenty feet below. The water was not very clear because even with the reef providing something of a barrier, it was pretty much open ocean. We could see about fifty feet in any direction, but I tried to look only ahead. My teeth chattered as I chomped down on the snorkel mouthpiece. I reasoned that if anything did attack, I would never know what hit me. I shivered, very afraid of dying, and tried not to let my imagination worm its way in, unaware that the trip out to the reef was the safer half of the expedition.

I left my anxiety behind as we reached the reef. The exhilaration of achievement, in hanging onto the sandstone and rock mounds, with corals and anemones, and myriads of sea life washing to and fro in the currents, quickly swept me into a dreamlike reverie. Albert explained that he would lead the way and point where he thought there'd be lobster or large fish hiding in the nooks and crannies of the rocks. He quickly speared a three pound grouper, which we put in my bag. (Ding ding.) Al tied it securely, enclosing the flopping, writhing creature. Then he pointed to a cave and made the gesture of antennae at his forehead indicating there could be lobster within. I eased forward, and slipped the looped, stiff wire of the snare over the smooth back of the lobster's carapace. When I felt the stiff wire slipping over the curled tail, I yanked hard, pulled the snare towards me, and pushed outward hard on the tube with my other hand to close the wire around the lobster's body. Al grabbed the thrashing lobster, stuffed it into his bag, and we continued the quest among the rocks until we had snared three more lobsters.

The wave action made it difficult to stay clear of the sharp corals and sea urchin needles. Even with the gloves and flippers which helped me grip and stabilize, scraped legs were unavoidable. Lacerations meant blood. Thrashing, wounded sea creatures made noise and leaked body fluids. We had snorkeled on the reef about twenty five minutes and it was time to head back to the beach. This time, it was impossible to avoid thoughts about sharks. Al said to make pounding, thumping surface noises with our fins if we spotted a shadow on the sandy bottom or a dark form in the waters.

Albert handed me the bag with the lobsters and he took both loaded spear guns and swam beside me. I let out the full length of line from both the net bags and pumped my legs with every ounce of energy I could muster. Adrenaline flowed as I tried not to picture catastrophe or imagine shadows. The mounting, rhythmic din of alarm bells synchronized with my pumping legs. A niggling question gnawed at me as to why *I* had the bags and *he* the spear guns, but terror now edged out any thought other than heading toward shore.

I held both lines in my one clenched fist, the sea water's steady resistance comforting as the net bags twirled behind me and I kicked my way toward shore. There was no way I would waste my energy looking around, and didn't want to see whatever might be out there anyway. About ten feet from the surf line, as I approached the beach, a steady tug seemed to pull that arm backwards and I yanked on it, imagination or not. I pumped mightily, swimming freestyle now, panicky, but still holding on to the line. Breaking through the surf, I tumbled onto shore, scrambling and clawing my way up the sandy incline. I stood up, heaved on the lines, and pulled with whatever strength I had left. Al popped out of the surf after me and clambered onto shore laughing and hooting. "He almost got one of the bags, the bastard, but you pulled it just in time."

I had mixed feelings about who was the real bastard. I flushed with pride for accomplishing such a daring exploit. At the same time, I felt like a fool for not confronting Al beforehand about something that seemed so rash and perilous. I had trusted this Albert Slaughter character, and figured with his experience in those waters, he would not willingly expose me to danger. Reason told me otherwise. Doubt whispered loudly and the clues mounted. But after such an unforgettable adventure, Al's Jacques Cousteau image remained untarnished for the time being.

We gave the grouper to the old couple for minding the car, and headed to San Juan. On the way back, before dropping me at the convent with three of the lobsters, Albert casually mentioned that if I had chickened out, he would not have continued all the way to the reef. He was amazed at my courage. I was amazed at my stupidity. The nuns were amazed at the surprise gift of lobster for their dinner.

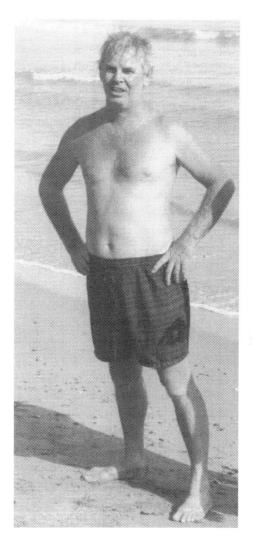

Albert in swim trunks at beach.

Chapter Twelve

1970 – 1978 Puerto Rico and New York

Once, On a High and Windy Hill

My first Christmas in Puerto Rico came. That is not something I can say I ever did with Albert.

He and I drove from the convent in San Juan to Cabo Rojo, a remote peninsula in Puerto Rico's southwest corner. Al's friend was the civilian lighthouse keeper hired by the Coast Guard to man a small lighthouse perched on a promontory. I had willingly accepted Albert's invitation to spend a few days there with him when he subbed for his friend during the holidays.

Blithely ignoring the obvious, I subsequently experienced an inglorious, lackluster honeymoon of sorts. I traded my virginity, along with any shred of personal integrity, for twelve years shared with Albert Slaughter It was a life woven of complex threads. A bit of Robinson Crusoe mingled with Jack Cousteau with a large swath of Gilligan and his island antics. It resulted in a tapestry whose motif revealed the dark side of the court jester. Lacking any sense of core self, I seemed to shape-shift in a Caribbean cautionary tale, with Al's unconscious fingers on the loom. Whatever role he woke up in the mood for, I played along as the sidekick.

I ignored the discomforting blips of alarm at Al's having been married four times, or that he was seventeen years my senior. He had admitted to an on-again, off-again drinking habit, and his close buddy even addressed him as a faggot. In my naiveté, I just thought it was very egalitarian of Albert to have once been roommates with one of the female impersonators in the Gala Revue at a tourist hotel.

When we returned from our holiday tryst at the lighthouse, I found on my desk a one-way airline ticket provided by the convent to get me back to New York and be effectively, "drummed out of the corps," that is, released from my vows. Sharpening my apprentice's skills in self-degradation, I gratefully used the ticket, once more passively allowing circumstances to dictate my next step in life.

"Cabo Rojo Lighthouse" (sketch by author)

I stayed for a month with my family in Douglas Manor, NY and in February was summoned to the motherhouse to meet with the convent "higher-ups." For years after, I considered it significant that I had signed the release papers from the bishop on Lincoln's birthday, February 12, 1971. It seemed my own emancipation proclamation, from a life of obeisance, although for years I had not faithfully lived the spirit of the vows of poverty, chastity, and obedience. And like many of the freed slaves who experienced an, "out of the frying pan and into the fire" life, mine, I sensed, would be a mixture of adventure mingled with strife and a growing lack of self worth and dignity. Characteristically nonchalant about it all, I used money from my father for the ticket back to Puerto Rico and to Albert E. Slaughter and the unknown.

My error was in perceiving it as a step toward freedom, while actually it was another piece of my lifelong pattern of avoiding responsibility and opting for someone else to provide a course of action, while I made my own hell within it. The "victim wannabe" was in full throttle to get back to Albert in Puerto Rico. I followed his lead, and "damn the consequences," if there was adventure to be had. Lonely confusion and tears of frustration followed soon after but I locked them into my own vortex of self-obliteration.

We lived for a bit in a rental in Isla Verde while Al helped finish the marine aquarium near the airport. For two months, I helped Albert in his work as foreman. We snorkeled in waters along Puerto Rico's coasts to gather reef fish, crustaceans, starfish, sand dollars, and corals, and even captured sharks to stock the tanks. The most fun was netting the seahorses as we snorkeled near the pilings of the bridges crisscrossing the lagoon between the Condado and Viejo San Juan. I became, "one of the guys." However, an embarrassingly memorable stench-filled event illustrates the depths of my approval-seeking conduct. One day, short on room in the cab of our van, I volunteered to lie in the walled back with the rotting carcass of a male sea lion. The unfortunate creature had died on route to Puerto Rico from Canada and had been donated to a UPR biology professor. I almost passed out, trying to breathe as little as possible on the twenty-minute ride. I had become a powerful master at generating experience to "prove" my unworthiness.

Still, I was in my own version of heaven for those months, tagging along on the snorkeling and SCUBA expeditions. Financial constraints and mismanagement however, forced the closing of the aquarium soon after it had finally opened. I was sorely disappointed, but had thoroughly enjoyed the underwater delight on the reefs and depths of Puerto Rico's coast. My youthful fantasies of following in the "fin steps" of Jacques Cousteau and Dr Eugenie Clark were coming to life.

But any chance of a satisfying sex life were dead in the water, when Al announced one evening in bed that he, "… didn't believe in foreplay." I was too unaware of sexual options at that point to express myself about it, but my body was not unaware of itself. My sleep was once again filled with dreams of women's bodies but I remained loyal to Al, and somewhat satisfied by his endless stories of exploits and the daily escapades we shared. That is, until I met Violette several years later.

Looking for Love in All the Wrong Places

The next two years we lived on Culebra, a tiny island to the northeast of the Puerto Rican mainland, where we managed a B&B for a Cuban fellow. We would teach guests to snorkel and take them out to spearfish or dive for conch for the dinner that night. Since we had few customers in those two years, we spent plenty of time diving for ourselves, exploring among the reefs in and around Culebra and its smaller outcrops of islands.

On one memorable trip we found ourselves snorkeling in a river-like current formed between two tiny islands. It wasn't too much of a struggle, yet we were distracted by the surreal carpet beneath us. Spent artillery shells of every description littered the sea bottom in the passage. There did not seem to be a square inch of natural sea floor. Small corals and sea fans grew among the steel debris. The strangeness of the scenario was compounded when we became completely enveloped in a school of barracuda which caught up with us and then slowed down to time their speed to ours. I was glad I did not sport any kind of flashing jewelry which might have sent them into a feeding frenzy. As it was, there seemed to be genuine curiosity in the myriads of eyes that accompanied us. We later discovered that the rocky islands had huge white bulls-eyes painted on them for the U.S. Navy pilots to use as practice in their air-to-surface maneuvers during their yearly "Operation Springboard."

Center: Sister Nan leaving for Puerto Rico
Clockwise, from top left: in Culebra, PR, Nan tossing shark
back into ocean; holding speared grouper; dismounted from her
horse, Lucero; and in Guayama, PR, harvesting eggplant.

I also had plenty of time to roam the island, riding bareback on my horse to remote areas to collect colorful seeds and gourds for crafts, or rambling over the cattle roads in our yellow Beetle. I explored pathways where I could scramble down cliff sides to hidden beaches to gather seashells, driftwood, and Japanese glass fishing buoys that washed ashore. It would have been idyllic except that in his boredom Al slid back into drinking, which loosened the restraints he had imposed on his attraction to young males. I spent many nights alone until he would appear days later, hung over, angry at himself, and filled with a silent rage. I wished I could tell him I really did not find a problem with his predilections. I certainly acknowledged to myself how comfortable I had always been about my sexuality and my own lust being stirred by both genders. I just did not know how to broach it with him because of his strict Southern Baptist upbringing. I sensed how much he loathed his activities. So I just left the subject unspoken and Albert himself to his discomfort. I ignored my loneliness, afraid that a frank discussion would sever our already tenuous relationship.

We had little money, but managed to eat by spear fishing on the nearby reefs and by trapping fresh water prawn in the hillside ponds. We wove the traps from the vines growing in nearby trees. Our meals were gourmet cuisine if you ignore the fact that we developed anemia and a vitamin A deficiency from the lack of red meat and fresh vegetables. We worked on a friend's fishing boat, trapping reef species like grouper, triggerfish, and parrotfish. We did long-lining for red snapper in the deeper waters off Culebra, and sold it all at the docks in St Thomas. At that time, the fish caught around St Thomas were known to have a nerve-affecting illness called ciquatera, so our catch from Culebran waters was eagerly awaited and sold out quickly. We made good money but Albert quickly squandered it on booze, boys, and a continuum of unfinished projects. I chose not to fret over this truth, knowing my own attraction to women. Happy to wander on the beaches and hillsides in solitary adventures, I was honing my skills in the mastery of misperception and self-delusion.

Gradually, Al grew bored. Under the pretext of an extended fishing trip to further waters, he deserted me in April 1972 and went back to the Puerto Rican mainland to work with his friend who was building a ferry. By the time I discovered he had left me, we had been evicted anyway. I

"Delusion in Paradise" (Sketch by author)

returned one day from my wandering, companionless but for my horse Lucero, to discover our meager belongings on the curb outside where the police had piled them.

My sister Rita had gotten married and was in St. Thomas on her honeymoon. She and her new husband, Bob, were supposed to fly over to Culebra to spend time with us. Mortified at my predicament, I scrounged up a few dollars to send a telegram to halt their visit. To this day, Bob still jokes about the look on their hotel receptionist's face at the ominous tone of the telegram. Strapped for cash, I had worded it as briefly as possible, so the aborted telegram read, *"Don't come to Culebra. Slaughter."* I was too proud to let my sibling know the dire straits I was in, or to what depths of unhappiness I had sunk. The energy of anxious defensiveness was still running me and I was not about to admit any error of judgment.

Confused and demoralized, I meekly traced Albert to Old San Juan and with very few words shared, I moved back in with him. I did not allow a glimmer of self-respect to surface, and chose to flippantly ignore any feelings of indignation. Where self-esteem might have dwelled there was only a void which made it possible for me to hollowly laugh it off.

I became a bar tender in Barry Navan's *Malamute Saloon*, a beer-and-shots-only joint on Calle Cristo. Al's friend, Barry, the very same ex-Navy diver who used to call Al a faggot to his face, was also an aficionado of Robert W. Services's ditties, and had named his two establishments for the poems. We lived in a back room of *Dangerous Dan McGrew's* and I worked in the other one a few blocks away. It catered to merchant seamen and to the older prostitutes, left behind when the Navy reduced their presence, or to an occasional male hooker who might wander in from the ranks of gays who prowled Calle Luna. I listened to many a tale and learned how universal the "victimhood and blame-game" is.

In April 1973, Albert and I sailed the home-built ferry down to the island of Martinique. A Frenchman had bought it to ferry workers across Fort de France Bay to the capital city. Once there, we spent a week exploring Martinique's fascinating pockets of natural beauty and history. We discovered a rum distillery that had been closed up since 1954 when the French brothers who owned it were killed in Vietnam at Dien Bien Phu. The white rum in the stainless steel tanks was still viable. The jackpot though, was the dark rum stored and aging in the gigantic oak casks, taller than Al and measuring eight full arms-lengths around. We heartily savored the mellowed, aromatic rum treasure. In the north, we explored a museum with artifacts and photos of the disaster in 1902 when Mt. Peleé exploded and in minutes had incinerated the city of Saint-Pierre and its 30,000 inhabitants. Another museum and grounds at Les Trois Islet was at the sugar refinery and homestead owned by the wealthy Creole family of Joséphine, the heart throb and wife of Napoleon Bonaparte.

The surface thrills were building in my life, but I allowed the deflation of self-worth and integrity to relentlessly drag me further out of balance. We did not just explore the island, we pilfered rum from the distillery, and hand-hewn tools from the open-air worksites at the Creole museum. It seems that the energies which fueled the furtive shoplifting and clandestine exploration in my youth and in the novitiate still ran deep. Ironically, many of these items were lost when the boat we sent them back on to Puerto Rico, sank in the Sir Francis Drake Channel in the British Virgin Islands. I too had sunk to new lows as I buried self-worth under a misdirected, desperate search for belonging even in a situation which brought little personal satisfaction.

After returning to Old San Juan, I managed a cigar and variety store on the cruise ship pier, selling mostly *Pepto-Bismol* and *Preparation H* to passengers who ate too much and exercised too little while cruising around the Caribbean. I fish-mongered from a homemade cart which my Doberman pinschers daily pulled to the Cataño Ferry Pier. I sold fresh fish and lobsters which a fisherman friend on Culebra sent over daily on the island-hopper flight. I also studied and interviewed with the Coast Guard to get my merchant seaman's card in the hopes of cooking and living on a friend's ferry in San Juan harbor.

Fickle as ever, Albert then wanted to actually marry me. How low could I get? It was in our cockroach infested room above the defunct barroom, *Dangerous Dan McGrew's*, that Al showed me the application from the Health Department. We would get the blood tests done and then had 28 days to either get married or start the process again.

Now well into my mastery of the vibrations of unworthiness and inadequacy, I thought it a lark that we spent the morning of the 28th day, a Sunday, driving around trying to find a place to get married. Al, at 47, and in his soiled work clothes, and I, a 30 year-old in jean cutoffs and tee shirt, made an improbable couple presenting ourselves at the municipal jail and night court down by the docks in Old San Juan. The magistrate was not above making an extra buck, so after determining that we were both functional in Spanish, with his secretary as the witness, he performed the civil marriage of Nan Walker. Burke and Albert Emerson Slaughter on June 15, 1973. The ring turned green after our next diving job. It pretty much had the same shelf life as our sexual relationship.

March 1976 – December 1978 Guayama, PR

Unconventional Oven

In early 1976, fed up with the bustle of the city and the fact that my car battery was stolen in front of the house when I parked for my 20-minute lunch break, I insisted we move to a rural area. Albert had been installing sea buoys for Pittsburg Plate Glass (PPG), a factory on Puerto Rico's southeast coast, and knew of land that was available. So for the next ten years, I got to live in a house we built on a Caribbean beach in Guayama, in a fishing barrio called Pozuelos. It was there that I homesteaded, raising pigs, ducks, chickens, and a cow, cultivated a vegetable garden and helped Al install and maintain channel-marking sea buoys.

I even discovered that it's possible to cook an entire red snapper within a compost heap. My friends ran a thoroughbred race horse breeding farm nearby. So I had a small mountain of fresh horse manure that was ripening for the vegetable garden. Each time I drove in or out of my compound, I noticed waves of heat undulating from the pile. I hatched a plan to cook something in it.

The next week, Al brought home a five pound red snapper that he'd caught while working on his friend's long-lining operation in the deep canyons a few miles offshore. The magic words were, "Hey hon, surprise me with a new way of cooking this, okay?" and off he went for the day to his many unfinished projects in the barrio.

It had already been cleaned and gutted. So I filleted the fish, rubbed a mixture of olive oil, lemon, minced garlic and onion, chopped oregano, salt and pepper onto both fillets and onto the fish skeleton. I tied the fish together with cooking string, laid some peeled, small potatoes and fresh carrot quarters around it, sprinkled more oil and condiments over everything, and wrapped it in many layers of heavy duty aluminum foil. I got a long handled shovel from the shed and dug a hole deep into the side of the manure heap. With the same shovel, I slid the fish package into its "natural as shit" oven, and repacked the hole tightly.

With no access to any information on the natural foods craze of the 70's, the "oven" timing was hit and miss. But five hours later, I triumphantly walked in with a fish wrapped in the innermost layer of foil. I had been careful to keep the outer layers outside, hidden from Albert's olfactory perusal. The meal was an overwhelming success, topped only by the look on Albert's face when I truthfully answered his question on how I managed to cook fish without the house smelling of it. We did not apply for a government patent on this method, but Al repeatedly bragged about it to anyone within earshot.

Playing God

The wretched dog swayed and painfully limped nearer the deep hole I had dug in the sandy yard. Trembling, he hesitated, but was drawn by the tidbit of meat I'd placed there. By the build, I guessed he had Lab or maybe Standard Poodle in him, but he had no hair. Scabbed skin draped on bones, his body reeked from the infected sores and scabbed over layers of skin. The stench of the scabies almost choked me but I bent down to place a large handful of hamburger meat near the rim. I was shaking too, my palms sweaty with apprehension. My stomach clenched as I reached for the shotgun I had borrowed. This was the first time I had ever used a gun. Unaware of my plans, Al had gone into town to the hardware store.

What if the bullet ricochets?

How many shots will kill him?

The dog started to cringe away so I gave him the last bunch of meat.

Will I know if he's truly dead?

Palm trees swayed in the breeze and Caribbean waves lapped at the shore in front of my house but the idyllic setting belied my anxiety and his instinctual mistrust. I was sick with disgust and fear. I was angry that people had dumped their pets near my house abandoning them so I would take them in.

Sorry I'm playing God, old fella but that's the way it is. I can't let folks take advantage of me. I've got to keep this under control.

His head was down gulping the sandy meat off the ground so I aimed at the back of his skull and squeezed the trigger. He slumped, legs buckling and fell into the hole, a chunk of his head blown off. My own four dogs were whining and I was crying as I filled in the grave. At least I could tell he was dead.

It'll be easier if there's a next time. Got to maintain control

Goslings and Rum

Violette, my French friend, lived on the mountain overlooking the bay behind my house. She was disappointed that her two Sebastopol geese mated regularly but the female would never sit on her eggs. So I put two fertilized eggs under my Muscovy ducks who were devoted sitters, timing it so I could sit beside the nest on the day each of them hatched. Voilà, I was imprinted on those tiny goose brains as "Mommy." Those little guys waddled and hopped after me everywhere, along with my dogs, a mother and son Doberman duo, and a mother and son German shepherd, My retinue trailed literally in my footsteps. Whether to pick eggplants and peppers from the garden, traipse through the sea grapes and dunes to the beach where the dogs always beat us down to the water line, or up and down the stairs to the house, we all traveled as a group.

The house was on anchored pilings, allowing the occasional storm surge to wash up harmlessly under the house. The dog door at the top of the stairs was in continuous use during the day. It also served as the perfect portal for the daily morning "alarm clock ritual." Around 6:00 am each day, after scouring the yard for bugs and ants, the two half-grown geese would clunk up the stairs, lurch pigeon-toed through the dog door, and plop in front of the full length mirror, preening themselves. The tap, tap, tapping on the mirror as they tried to reach their reflections was an amusing and comforting wake-up routine.

One morning, ominous silence greeted me. No tapping, no clunking or soft quacking murmurs. I ran downstairs to their hutch where both of them were stretched out on the straw, weakly moving their legs, trying to stand up but with necks and heads flopping in the grit. There was no sign

Goslings following Nan.

of an intruder, no blood, only lolling heads and silence. I picked up each one and gave it mouth to mouth resuscitation several times. I figured with their labored breathing, it was something respiratory, so I gave my version of avian CPR. I put a few drops of water into each of their mouths, and to one of them I gave a drop of Barrrilito rum. By the afternoon, one of the baby geese had succumbed but the other seemed to be recovering. It was empty comfort that it was the little guy who got the rum who made it through the ordeal.

Throughout the day I worried about what was really going on. Was it some kind of botulism from the "swimming hole" I made for them out of a forty gallon drum? I had put some plants in it from the river, so maybe there *was* some kind of bacteria they ingested or that got through their skin. Then my imagination started taking over,

Oh god, maybe now I'm infected. I had my mouth over their beaks, such a dumbbell!

I was going to a New Year's Eve party that night.

I'm going to spread some kind of botulism all over the barrio, 'cause, of course I'll be kissing everybody at the party!

I hopped in my truck and drove into town to the local clinic, which I hoped was open on New Year's Eve day. There was one nurse receptionist, and by some miracle I was the only client. She made me wait for what I guess she deemed an appropriate amount of time, to show me that *she's* in charge here and not *I,* and addressed me in Spanish, asking what my problem was. I responded in Spanish, "Pués, mire, esta mañana, mis dos gansitos estaban muy graves. Pués, uno se murió y el otro ya vive, pero está muy enfermo todavía …" I continued a mile a minute in Spanish, telling her my tale of woe and that I was afraid I would spread botulism because I had given mouth to mouth resuscitation to my baby geese.

I never got to the end. As I gushed on, still in Spanish her eyes were getting wider and wider. Her shoulders were heaving, and her head was down and away from me. Gasping, trying not to laugh out loud, she turned around and shouted in Spanish to someone in the next cubby, "Oh my god, you have *got* to hear this one's Spanish! It's *so* bad that it's coming out like she just gave mouth to mouth resuscitation to some baby geese! I don't know what kind of dictionary she's using, but somebody *really* played a good joke on her!" They both burst out laughing, no not laughing, squealing, then ripping it out. They *rolled* on the floor practically.

The doctor came out to see what the hullabaloo was about. The one nurse could hardly speak, but in Spanish, in between gasps, she managed to squeeze out something about my horrendous Spanish and that it sounded like geese, and mouth to mouth resuscitation, and rum, and botulism … "Doctor, talk to her in *English, OK?*"

On our way to his office he slowly and patronizingly said in English, "So tell me in English what your problem is today." I began again, but this time I gave the streamlined version, running on in rapid fire, "Well, this morning, my two baby geese were very ill with something respiratory, so I gave each of them mouth to mouth resuscitation. One died, but the one I gave the rum to survived, and now I'm worried that I could spread some kind of botulism if I kiss people at the party tonight because I may have gotten some bacteria from their mouths, if that's what made them sick." Now *he* was wiping tears from his eyes and rocking back and forth in the chair. He jumped up, ran to the door and called to the nurses in the front office to tell them that my Spanish was just fine. When he got composed again he sat down, laughed, and answered, "No, I think you can kiss folks, to ring in the New Year. You're not going to spread anything."

Then he leaned toward my face peering at my eyes and said, "But tell me are your eyes always this bloodshot?" At my answer in the affirmative, he wrote out the name of some eye drops and a prescription. I thanked him and asked what the fee was.

"Ma'm," he blurted, "I owe *you* actually. This is one of the wackiest stories I've ever heard and I'm going to have something to tell at parties around here for years to come. But why don't you go home and see if that other goose actually did survive that premium rum you gave it!"

It was a happy ending for all. I enjoyed the party. The surviving goose took up residence at Violette's with its real parents. And the four dogs didn't have to wait each time, for me to get down to the beach to toss a coconut into the waves for them.

Red, Right, Returning

For a man who had completed school only through the seventh grade when his father made him work in a factory during the Depression, Al was creatively inventive. He read voraciously and delighted in discussing a wide range of topics. I had encouraged and helped him to get his GED. He actually studied and passed the whole thing in Spanish.

He was an observant entrepreneur and had noticed that the U. S. Coastguard regularly dumped sea buoys at a scrap yard near the docks. Most of them had been surveyed out of service because of rust holes. We would buy the buoys from the scrap heap for pennies on the pound, fill them with polyurethane foam, then fiberglass and gel-coat them. The Coast Guard actually agreed to test one of our refurbished buoys for five years in the waters near St. Thomas. Albert gallantly gave both our names as co-inventors on a U. S. Patent for our method of refurbishing ocean buoys. We would outfit them with battery packs from Texas Instruments, and compete with major marine installation companies for the contracts to install buoys to mark the harbor entry channels along Puerto Rico's coastline. Government power plants and private industry needed their entry channels clearly marked and our bids of $150,000 or so, usually beat the competition at their three or four hundred thousand dollar bids. Our profits were enormous.

We could underbid the major companies because of our homespun methods. We jerry-rigged a way of using local fishermen's outboard powered rowboats to ferry the floating buoys out to their locations. The buoy anchors were several old engine blocks encased in cement "coffins" of wood. The sea chains were securely implanted in that cement conglomeration. We would securely bunch together the buoy, cement block, and chain floating within a "tire" flotation device and hanging between two dories with outboards. At the point designated by the Coast Guard, the chain and anchor were allowed to sink and the buoy was secured and ready for activation The battery packs were calibrated according to the sea lane charts and their "seconds on-seconds off" timing of the blinking lights. We usually would also get a multi-year contract to maintain the buoys for the factory or government enterprise that had contracted our installation services. Albert E. Slaughter, with his dirth of formal education but a depth of street smarts and an expansive, *bon vivant* personality, taught me that, "If you look in charge, you *are* in charge." I carried that assuring nugget through much of my later adult life.

I had become his fifth wife, and was interested only in merry escapades. But after eight years with Al, my maternal instincts reared their hormonal head. The apprenticeship to illusion had blossomed to near mastery by now. I had become skilled in the ability to focus only on the moment of upbeat fun or the daring exploit while ignoring a feeling of being buried under the increased ease of self-deception.

Nature or Nurture

I walked on the beach in front of our house in Guayama, with our friends, Alejandro and Marta, Spanish flamenco dancers who performed in a San Juan hotel. Their three-year-old son, Tomás, called Tosho, happily marched and splashed ahead of us. His curly, dark hair blew in the breeze, while his arm draped affectionately over the shoulders of my "son," Big Red, a large, affable red Doberman. But in those moments on the beach, watching Tosho, I felt a lurch in my innards and a longing I didn't recognize.

Two of my three sisters, and my sister-in-law, were pregnant. I was thirty-four years old, living my Jacques Cousteau-like dream. Albert and I had our own business installing and maintaining the sea buoys which marked the shipping lanes for government and private companies with facilities on the south coast of Puerto Rico. We lived in a house we'd built in front of the Caribbean Sea. Our family consisted of the four dogs, two cats, and the two baby geese which followed me everywhere. After having four children in quick succession as a very young and lusty husband, Al had opted for a vasectomy twenty years before. I felt relieved, because no one in his family could handle alcohol, especially Albert himself, and fine spirits were a staple in mine. I didn't want that gene of his passed to my child. But I hadn't recognized until then, the empty place in my heart.

Almost frozen in my tracks, with my belly clenched around a now unwelcome emptiness, I realized how much I ached for a baby. Adoption didn't appeal; I wanted to experience childbirth. I felt amazed, albeit uncomfortably, at my willingness to imitate my sisters. I had spent a lifetime being different, walking a rebel's path, choosing for the moment, and living recklessly. Now I just wanted to join the clan, add to it, and proudly march with it. I hurtled forward with my usual abandon.

I drove into town and called my sister, Rita, a pediatric nurse, with two boys, four-and two-years-olds, and expecting her third child. She suggested artificial insemination and gave me the name of a clinic in Queens County, New York, with its own sperm bank. They advised me to track my fertility cycles with a basal thermometer and keep records of my body temperature when I woke up each morning. I methodically started in March 1977, and with my three months of a stable cycle tracked, I planned to fly to New York for insemination at the clinic.

I made an appointment with the clinic for a time in August when I'd have that window of two or three days of optimum fertility for insemination. Meanwhile, I perused the clinic's surreal shopping list of possible physical characteristics for my child. I specified a donor of northern European, possibly Scandinavian descent, with blond hair, blue eyes, and skin that tanned. I ordered a slim build and athleticism, but emphasized that intelligence was paramount, a PhD preferable.

In late August, 1977, I lay on my back on the clinic's table, alone, by my own choice. Legs in stirrups, I awaited the actual insemination. I tingled with anticipation, excited about the impending possibilities, but not entirely convinced of the wisdom in this approach to motherhood. Something niggled at me but I couldn't identify the origin of my disquiet. Refusing to back down from my months of planning and record-keeping, I plunged ahead, (as did the doctor.). He squirted in the "donation," and instructed me to lie there for half an hour to allow the sperm to run their age-old marathon, in optimal, unimpeded competition towards the golden prize, my egg.

That evening, in a Japanese restaurant with my cousin and his wife, an unmistakable odor of seminal fluid pervaded the air at our table. It hovered around me like the stale stench that wafted out of the public men's room in Manhattan's Central Park. I wore it as my badge of honor, however, and with the pride of accomplishment. My cousin and his wife, aware of my clinic appointment, never made reference to the one-night-stand motel aroma. I ordered a fish entrée in a futile attempt at disguise.

During the night, in bed, as I reviewed the day's momentous nature, the source of my earlier misgivings on the clinic table resolved itself into striking clarity. The sperm bank's wish list had no "Sense of Humor" category. I realized with perfect, innate certainty that I would never willingly hang out with anyone who didn't have a sense of humor. Why would I want to have a child with a person whose comedic acumen was not evident?

My family thrived on wit. We delighted in pointing out the paradoxical or incongruous. Word games amused us and the plays on words, evident in English and other languages, provided a source of great sport. Laughing had turned many a sibling dispute into a rollicking, jovial moment. I had stayed with Al through the years because of his wit and penchant for a joke or a humorous tale. I decided not to take a chance getting a sperm donor who couldn't remember a punch line. I lay there almost hoping that this first attempt would not take, or at least, if there were a victorious sperm, that it would carry a gene or two from the clown in the guy's family tree.

The next day, instead of staying in the States another month for the clinic's second attempt, I returned home, determined to sort through our friends and acquaintances and target a donor dad. Sense of humor came first, followed by as many of the other requisites as possible. Thus began my crusade. With total disregard for the sacred integrity of other people's families, I forged ahead in my quest to start my own. Like the crusaders, I turned a blind eye to the possible havoc I might wreak upon the lives of others as I aimed my sights on reclaiming "holy" territory: my chance at motherhood. My personal Holy Grail overflowed with jovial, prancing sperm, laughing and tumbling their way to the brim.

I didn't tell Albert about my search plans. I admitted only that I had recriminations about humorless progeny, but still wanted to have a baby. Nothing much else was said, but after eight years together, we had developed a tacit understanding of each other's vagaries. Al had told me to begin a search and that is what I did. I had chosen a spouse who operated with the same laissez-faire approach to me as had my parents. Mastery of the energies of covert manipulation and arrogant disregard for others was being achieved, it seems.

Al and I lived on a spit of land that formed a barrier beach of sorts, and hemmed in a bay behind us to the north. Our beach was a favorite of the engineers and their families from the States who lived in the town of Guayama, and worked five year stints at the various plants on Puerto Rico's south coast. We had met several of the families as they strolled the beach and through them, became acquainted with many more. Potential sperm bank donors abounded among the intelligent men we knew. I tried to winnow it down to my specific criteria and, of course, to the main ingredient – that precious mirth. I spent September and October surveying my prospects, pondering over my choices, observing the men more closely. I zeroed in on cheerfulness; my antennae captured any notes of merriment or jests.

My search narrowed to two men. We were close to both families, and had frequently invited them to beach parties and pig roasts in our barrio. We'd go to their homes in town for family celebrations and card games. I finally decided that one of the men was too Catholic to even consider it. The other fellow fit the criteria perfectly, considering that the now limited field forced me into a much wider margin for error. Arnold was a free spirit and I figured he could handle the fact that I didn't want any fatherly attitude from him or attachment to the child, once I might become pregnant.

When I approached him about the deal, he had his own proposition. He counter-offered that if I were willing to trade in the turkey baster, to do it the good old fashioned way, he'd acquiesce to my "no strings attached" demand. I had no objections, considering Al's "declaration of war" on foreplay. Our already sub-par lovemaking had nosedived, and to my chagrin, it wasn't his nose down there. I gave him hand jobs; he told me old Navy jokes. I was ripe for a man who actually enjoyed sex with a woman. Arnold, known to friends as Nolly, agreed to "come" for three days in succession during each month's window of opportunity. His lunch break wasn't the only thing he'd extended.

During the six months of attempts, we creatively used a variety of meeting places, and made delicious use of our carte blanche efforts to make a baby. It was not a romance or a fling. I was fixated on becoming pregnant and had absolutely no designs on Nolly, body or soul. I was strictly "borrowing" his sperm. Although in hindsight, that was a ridiculous notion considering there was no way of "returning" it. It was my slick ticket to motherhood. For the first time since my convent days of lovemaking with Sister Lucy Marie, I left each tryst sated, and tingling with anticipation for the next rendezvous. I selfishly ignored any subconscious hint that I might be infringing on the rights of another woman, who in fact was a kind friend of mine, and would subsequently prove more so once I became pregnant.

Nolly's boat was a favorite spot, and the subterfuge I'd practiced so artfully as a youth, served me well. Few things remained secret in a Puerto Rican barrio. I reasoned that since Al proved gracious enough to give me slack in this enterprise, I wouldn't insult his pride. Also, I certainly did not want Nolly's wife to be aware of his lunchtime "extra duty." It was enough for me that if Nolly and I agreed to meet at his boat, I made sure to trek through the marshes rather than drive in full view down the yacht club road. Once I'd snuck onto the boat and down into the cabin, Nolly puttered out into the middle of the bay. We could at least enjoy ourselves out there in relative privacy.

One time, we met in my former farmhouse down the road, but the occasional passing vehicle made me nervous and I did not conceive. We coupled in his truck hidden in a cane field during the *cosecha* (harvest) season. I found it hard to concentrate, knowing that acres of cane fields were routinely set on fire before the actual cutting commenced. I imagined the gossip about the *"coitus interuptus by the flammae eruptus."* I saw newspaper headlines, *Americanos caught "in flagrante" in the conflagration.*

I blithely ignored the fact that this man was married. In fact, when we weren't engaged in our monthly trysts, I socialized with his wife, Allie, along with some of the other engineers' wives. What started as my reconnaissance mission to find a possible donor, became a full "blown" Green Beret "penetration campaign," and I got into commando mode whenever my monthly body rhythms dictated. I wanted to become pregnant, and did not allow myself to consider either his or her feelings. I never asked him if he had discussed it with her. I was so driven by a quest for motherhood that I didn't seem to care. If this was amoral behavior, I ignored any signals sent by my conscience. To me it was a case of using his sperm, no more, no less. In my mind, it had nothing to do with relationship or exclusivity. Once again, my arrogant disregard for others ran rampant.

In the sixth month of programmed endeavors, I got pregnant. We had moored his boat in the middle of the bay, eaten a tasty lunch, and gone skinny dipping, diving off the boat into the warm, translucent waters. When Nolly treated me to underwater oral sex, I gurgled my undulating version of a big-eyed orphan's "Cavortin' Chameleons!" This Daddy Spermbuck's largess had left Albert's "no foreplay" disposition back at the orphanage. I don't know if it was the hours of languid fondling in the water, or the glistening, soaking-wet oral sex later in the boat, but we delivered a *coup de grace* to my childless existence.

The doctor delivered too. On Christmas Day in 1978, two weeks early and not quite immaculately conceived, but certainly messianic to me, my daughter Virginia Fay was born. Albert never asked a thing about the specifics. Not only did he graciously sign the birth registration, but he began strutting through the barrio crowing about fathering this beautiful child in his "dotage." It was Nolly's genes though, that joined with mine in the marvelously perceptive and fun-loving sense of humor that Virginia Fay displayed, even from a very young age. Among the many positive traits that she inherited from him, it is that one for which I especially thank Nolly. On an ironic note, the only friends who came to the hospital to visit the new baby were Nolly and his wonderful wife, my friend Allie.

We called the baby "Fay" for Albert's mother who had passed away, since the two "Virginias," my mother and sister, were still alive and well. Fay proved to be a water child. After conception in, or on, the bay, she grew within me for those nine months in the beach house, as I snorkeled and body surfed well into the seventh month, and strolled the beach for miles, at least three times a day.

Ironically, it was the kind, selfless caring of Nolly's wife, Allie, which nursed me through a five-week bout of bed rest when I began to bleed after body surfing with friends when nearly eight months pregnant. She came by our phoneless beach house to visit one rainy day only to discover me in bed and the place a shambles. Albert had gotten in trouble with the law and was cooling his heels in the local jail. I was immobilized and abed, the dogs unfed, and the house rank with damp, unwashed laundry. She efficiently tidied up, and organized a food chain among our mutual friends until Albert got his situation straightened out. If it had not been for her kindness, unknown to her, her husband's child might not have survived my foolish "elderly prima parta" water sport escapades so late in the final term.

It serves to highlight how juxtaposed we two women were, I in ruthless pursuit of a goal, heedless of moral and physical consequences, and she, somewhat younger, but way wiser in her caring concern. Our pathways had twisted and then converged in these unusual circumstances, each of us following the heart's urgings.

As for Al and his new chance at family life, what followed was for him a blend of endearing, wise fathering and booze-filled episodes of self loathing. I found myself hovering between heart-swelling happiness and walking on egg shells. With his large and generous heart, Albert, though not her biological father loved Virginia Fay dearly. We each called her Fay but Al often used "Fay Marine." He had renamed his business "Fay Marine Services" for her. He doted on her and strutted around the barrio with her, offering his "personal services," should any fisherman's wife want a blue-eyed, blond-haired "gringa-Rican"

So Fay, this water baby, floated through her first week of life wide eyed, in tide pools in front of the house, the very same sandy basins where the sight of three-year-old Tosho had first caused that stirring in my loins. She spent her first five years in front of the Caribbean Sea, with the sound of surf gently ebbing and flowing in constant rhythm, night and day. Water aside, most importantly to me, be it nature or nurture, Virginia Fay has a formidable repertoire of jokes, and she never forgets a punch line. Through the years, she and I have talked at length about the fact that she has two daddies, and later on, two mommies. She jokes about it and insists she is not bothered, but rather considers herself especially blessed and knows she was definitely wanted.

**Three photos: Nan pregnant, baby in surf with Nan
and Sandy, baby in surf with Albert.**

Top: Nan's parents and Fay; Sandy and Peter on our fishing boat with Fay;
Middle: Nephews and Fay on our fishing boat; Fay in front of our house;
Bottom: Ayn Kelly and Al with 9 mos. old Fay, snorkeling;
Al and 18 mos. old Fay holding spiny lobster

Top: Nan, newborn Fay, Albert, Nan's mother,
Virginia; Al, Fay, and puppy Warlock;
Bottom: Al bathing Fay with Blackjack's help; Al comforting Fay

Segment IV

1981 – 2006

Still Embracing the Illusion of Victimhood

William the donkey inspecting Fay's Fisher-Price plastic letters.

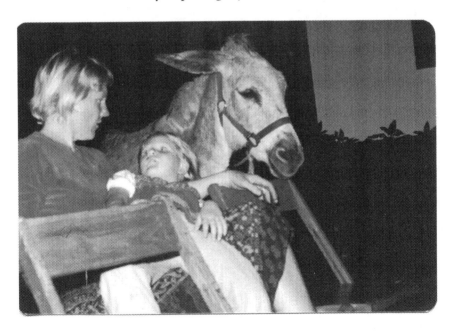

Nan and Fay sharing quiet moment with William at Violette's parties.

Chapter Thirteen

Putting the Finishing Touches on the Maze Construction

Mixed Messages

Two year-old Fay and I were frequent visitors at my French friend, Violette's, menagerie in the mountain foothills behind our beachfront barrio. She shared her zoo-like compound with her husband, teenage son, and a raucous assortment of donkeys, horses, a pair of Capuchin monkeys, a mynah bird, ducks, geese, and two mammoth German shepherds. Violette was an intrepid steward of her flock, even to the point of carting most of these two and four-legged creatures twenty miles away to her husband's office complex one September when a hurricane threatened her area.

We often would have picnics down the beach from my house with baby Virginia Fay, my four dogs, and her two mammoth German shepherds. Visits to her home in the hills were an all-day culinary delight and animal park adventure. Sometimes, we'd have lively parties at her place where her donkey William, freely wandered, filching from people's plates and trying to nibble at Fay's Fisher-Price plastic letters she played with on the ground. Violette's two Capuchin monkeys, Moe and Shlomo, no longer had free range because they had grown too jealous of Violette's affections directed elsewhere, so they swung about, chattering and screaming in their huge hillside pens. This formed a raucous counterpoint to Merlin, the myhna bird's shrill imitations of various bits of conversation. Life in our corner of the world was never dull.

Actually, it was the amusing fun with Merlin that inspired me to take a trip across the mountains to the north coast to buy a mynah bird for myself. When Violette and I arrived at the pet shop in Santurce, with Fay in tow, I met with a dazzling array of bird choices. The room seemed electrically charged with the ear-piercing calls of every shape and color of avian offerings. But as I walked up and down the cage area, I grew increasingly attracted to a particular creature, about thirteen inches long from bright red tail to light gray head, who seemed to be playing "hide and seek" with me. I was lured by a bobbing gray head with curved black beak, pearly grayish eyes set in bright white patches on either side of the head, and dark pupils which boldly stared at me. This creature toyed with my sense of playfulness, edging me into her game. The bird seemed to be steadily purring, like a happily contented cat. I was hooked.

When I inquired about the bird, the shop owner came over quickly and made an offer I could not refuse.

"Not only will I give you this bird for the price it cost me, but I will throw in a year's worth of food restocking credit, a sturdy cage, and any accessories you want."

Before I could utter a response, he continued with exasperation, "This Houdini bird is responsible for at least two other parrots escaping through the front door, and for this," and he held up an index finger with a still angry-looking scar, barely healed and still oozing a bit.

I'm already thinking, *I really like this bird. Sounds like my kind of fun.* Then he goes on with the story. Apparently, shortly after the arrival of this particular bird, the helper opened up the store one morning, and as he came in the front door, two small parrots flew out into the city streets, one an Electus and the other a Senegal, both of which were brightly colored, good talkers, and fairly pricey. It cost the owner any profit he may have made with a "higher than usual turnover rate" kind of bird. The interior of the store was swarming with birds flying freely, pooping everywhere, and causing the store to close down for the day to capture the birds and sort them back into proper cages. The owner quietly stayed within the back of the store that night and witnessed this African Gray (my African Gray, now in my mind) cleverly manipulating its way out of its own cage. It deliberately approached the community cage where it worked at the clip from the outside. Before the parrot could release the latch on the big cage full of birds, the owner swooped down on the African Gray with a net. He promptly brought it to the back room where he clipped a wing to prevent the bird from flying.

Since that incident, the African Gray had been sold twice but was returned by each disgruntled buyer with the claim that it was vicious, sullen, or too quiet, with no ability to talk. The whole time the owner was talking, the bird used its closed beak to caress my finger that I had placed up to the cage wire. We were pals already.

Violette and I, with Fay in the back, drove the two hours home over the mountains, the three of us serenaded by an assortment of whistles, clicking, whirring, purring, and soft murmuring from "Smokie," now officially name-approved by Virginia Fay. "Smokie" sported a large white patch around each pearly eye, soft gray coloring on her body feathers each of which was scalloped in whitish gray. Her wings were a darker gray and her crowning glory was her bright red tail feathers. She was as talented an African Gray parrot as there ever was and proved to be a real pal. A more appropriate name might have been Lazarus Houdini Berlitz because of the escapades she either created or endured. 1981 to 1986 was a brief moment in the 50 to 70 year lifespan of an African Gray but for me that charming interlude was replete with her mischievously intelligent antics and the mutual trust that we built between us.

I placed the large cage in the open-spaced family room and kept Smokie there until she became used to the family rhythms and activities. Albert, ever agreeable to any of my projects and pursuits, soon engaged Smokie in conversation, though decidedly one-sided. But that aspect quickly developed into conversational amusement for everyone.

She eventually was able to imitate his voice perfectly. It was so much so, that one morning, after Al had left the house for a day's work up in San Juan, exiting with the usual, "See you later on, hon," I was startled an hour later to hear him say his usual arrival greeting, "Hi honey, I'm home." I answered from the back room, "What happened? Car trouble? You're back so soon." There was no response for a while, then came another Albert greeting, "Hi honey, I'm home." I called again, walking out of the back, when Al's voice again called, "See you later on, hon," and I laughed to see there was no Albert. There was only Smokie, munching on a shard of carrot.

After her normal molt cycle, a bloody feather stump worked its way out of her clipped wing and she grew in her flight feathers. I had been allowing her out of the cage during the day, careful to keep the screen door securely locked, to prevent escapes by both Fay and Smokie. Using furniture, wall hangings, and any inventive route she discovered, the bird could climb up onto the rafters of our post and beam house and walk freely along the thick rafters, fluttering her way back down when she wanted. Then with her flight feathers in, she had full liberty to fly around the spacious main room and up onto the rafters and the tops of the bedroom walls.

It was a handy place from which she could survey the activities of the four dogs, the two cats, and Fay, Albert and myself. There was no question, as to who ruled the roost in our home. While Smokie was in the house, she inspected and approved of any feeding routines for the cats and the dogs. She was fearless with the mother and son Doberman duo, and a mother and son German shepherd. As soon as the bowls were placed on the floor, Smokie would silently swoop down to the floor, strut deliberately over to each bowl, try some food, and flutter or strut to the next. The dogs and cats learned from painful experience to patiently endure the inspection process before each one of them carefully edged towards their respective bowls. She would sometimes remain among them while they ate, or otherwise return to her own feeding or lookout post. It was quite a sight to witness large dogs and feisty cats being intimidated by a walking, talking twenty two ounce package of gray feathers.

One of her very amusing mimicry routines involved all the perfectly executed sounds of the Spanish-speaking workers, the dogs, Al's voice, and the banging wooden screen door. Most mornings, for a long stretch of time, Albert had a crew of local workers from the barrio helping him on a building project. The men would arrive early each morning calling up to Al, in Spanish, to come down to where they were waiting below the house's raised pilings. The dogs would start a raucously barking episode at this loud, sudden disturbance of the peace. Al would respond in Spanish to yell at the dogs and to tell the guys he was coming. Then he would kiss me and Fay goodbye and exit with his usual, "See you later on, hon," and go out the screen door, letting it slam behind him.

African Gray parrot, Smokie, and her antics

Smokie eventually got the entire routine together, imitating sections, trying them out, and finally entertaining us with a multilingual, Spanish, English, canine, and wooden door slam performance that could have won the grand prize on some TV entertainment program. When the mood struck her she would spontaneously burst into a strong rendition of, "Gringo! Gringo! Estámos aquí, esperándole. Vente, gringo, vente!" Then multiple barking sounds would follow. The air was rent with sharp bow-wows, low, growling ruffs, repeated high-pitched arf arfs, and booming woof woofs. Al's determined disciplining shouts would intervene. "Cayense, cayense," (Shut up, shut up) would be followed by his loud acknowledgment to the men, that he was coming, "Ya voy, ya voy." A final door slamming sound would punctuate the whole routine, followed by a blessed silence. It was hilarious and Smokie seemed to bask in the attention of the appreciative laughing. She knew whenever there was an audience and would launch a performance to suit the mood. She was very intelligent.

Eventually, I built a walk-in cage in the yard, one side against the back wall of the house. It was ten feet tall, sixteen feet long, and eight feet wide, with room for her to fly and perch on large sections of driftwood, and had passion fruit vines growing across the outside of the top, with some of the fruit growing inside for her.

She spoke French also, through the influence of my friend Violette, so each morning when I uncovered the cage if she was inside the house, or when I walked into the outside cage if she stayed there that night, she would say with perfect cadence and accent, "Bonjour, bonjour. Comment ça vas?" (Good morning, good morning. How's it going?) At night, when I placed the sheet over the cage indoors, I would say, and she would repeat, "Bonne nuit. Fais de beaux reves." (Good night. Sweet dreams.) This was the same if I placed her in the outdoor cage for the night, and walked out and away. She was very responsive for the appropriate phrase or routine.

After a year or so, I would allow her to fly away into the barrio each day. She would perch on my shoulder until we were outside, and when I said, "Au revoir," (See you!) she would fly off into the neighborhood with a parting, "Au revoir," heading out along the beach. Near sundown, she would return, land in the flamboyán tree next to the house and exclaim, "Je suis arrivée." (I am arrived/ I'm back.) Even with the loyalty of four loving dogs, I had never enjoyed such mutually trusting companionship as I had with Smokie, this African Gray parrot I was privileged to steward.

Primal Rage Awakened

I had developed a gall bladder condition, but the U.S. Public Health system was undergoing a dismantling by Reaganomics. With my Merchant Marine status, I was being flown to New York's Staten Island facility, to the last remaining operating room still accepting patients.

I planned to drive up from Guayama to the north coast outside of San Juan, where my sister, Rita was staying with her four young children. Her husband was an internal auditor for the federal government and worked temporarily in San Juan. I was going to leave Virginia Fay with her while I was in New York for the operation. I did not want to leave her with Al because I feared his vindictiveness and did not trust him being a reliable caretaker at this point. Violette had already taken my African Gray parrot, Smokie, up to her menagerie in the hills.

The night before I was to go, Al was sitting on one side of the big living area and called to two-year-old Fay who was sitting with me in the hammock on the far end. She scrambled out of the hammock and eagerly scooted across the room to him, arms outstretched. As she approached him, he roughly shouted at her,

"Get away from me!"

She scampered back to me whimpering in frightened bewilderment. I stood up from the hammock and called out, asking why he'd acted so viciously.

"Do you still want that divorce?" he scowled.

"Yes, I do," I quietly answered.

He retorted, "Then I'm going to hurt you any way I can."

When it had just been myself, I could handle his meanness as a drunk. Motherhood though, had awakened in me an inner strength and a protective awareness. I slowly and deliberately sidled over to him. My body energetically became a bastion of massive proportions. I inexorably inched my way against him, forcing him to the wall. He was taller than I, but in the internal primal scream of the outraged mother, I became volcanically protective in a smoldering menace of quiet force. I managed to place my face against his and in barely suppressed rage, eye to eye, cheek to cheek with him, I slowly gurgled,

"If you *ever* hurt this child again, in *any* way, I will wait until you are asleep and I will *slit your throat* ... with your own diving knife."

Eyes still locked on his, as a wary animal guardedly backs away from a potential threat, I released my energy-only grip on Al and both our bodies retreated to our own stances, although he still seemed melded to the wall. Voicelessly he grabbed the car keys from their perch and threw them out the door into the night air.

"Now try to leave," he mumbled, as he stalked down the stairs and drove away in his truck, gone for the night.

The next morning, I had to go down into the barrio to ask one of the fishermen to drive me up to my sister's house and then to the airport. That must have been how Albert was able to track his way to my sister's three days later, retrieve Virginia Fay, and bring her back down to Pozuelos. He then deposited her with another fisherman's family while he went off on his escapades. The folks in the barrio were always kind and caring, yet I will never know what actually transpired in childcare. But I still feared for my young daughter's sensibilities, confused and frightened as she had been. I too, was quite traumatized, and ill from a gall bladder that I was told had been atrophied for probably a year. I had to convalesce at the hospital and at another sister's home, for nearly a month, with no knowledge or control of my young daughter's wellbeing.

I had drawn these experiences to myself, energetically convinced of my unworthiness of anything better. The world I was generating "proved" yet again that I was not worth being counted among the respected. I had not yet opened to the Comforter Within. It is a testament to Virginia Fay's resilient character and indwelling wise voice that she weathered the vibrations of turmoil around her. She managed not only to grow in core strength but to also keep intact her marvelous, lighthearted sense of humor.

Gray Bird, Gray Clouds

One day in early 1983, Fay and I had gone out first thing in the morning for a day of shopping and visits, and had left Smokie in the house. Her indoor cage was always left open so she had free range of the house. The dogs were out in the fenced back yard. I came home with Fay in the early afternoon and was greeted by clearly agitated dogs and a suspiciously quiet house. Inside, occasional gray feathers lay scattered on the floor under two different rafters. More alarmingly, there were various small objects and pillows on the floor, and dishcloths hanging on wall decorations which themselves were askew. Then I saw the big frying pan on the stovetop with a feathered imprint on the greasy pan surface and two gray feathers stuck in the grease. Whoever came in and took Smokie must have been tossing things at her to impede her flight. Apparently, they succeeded when she was knocked down into the grease of the breakfast's fried bananas. I was too frantic to check on whatever else was gone, but nothing mattered to me anyway, except Smokie.

The ground outside the yard was filled with horses' footprints. Most local horse owners didn't shoe their horses because they ride them sporadically and usually keep to the dirt paths and beaches. The trail led down the path out front and clearly showed that two horses had come up from the east along the beach to the house and had returned that way. Nobody from up that way in the neighborhood had horses. Since the whole neighborhood and fishing village barrio was on a peninsula from east to west with the beach to the south, there was only one thought nagging at me. Somebody from Jobos, a hamlet around the swamp and across the bay to the north must have come looking for trouble.

Occasionally teenage boys would come along the beach on their horses from that direction and would nose around curiously. I would always greet them and chat in Spanish but the dogs would put up such a fuss that we never got into establishing any friendships and they always moved on down the beach to the west. Albert and I were very interactive in the barrio where we lived and we had great friendships with the families. People came and went freely and the whole neighborhood was always invited to our pig roasts and celebrations. We had never experienced any problem since moving here from San Juan in 1976. But the kids from Jobos seemed to be a different lot. There was some known petty crime, and it was more extensively populated than our little neighborly peninsula/fishing village. Someone must have been told of, or seen Smokie on my shoulder or in the neighborhood on one of her daily forays.

Albert was spending more time up in San Juan since I had by now, filed for divorce and we were technically separated even though still both living in the house. So I went into town with Fay to report the incident to the police. They didn't come out right away, but things being a bit relaxed in that part of the world, they told me the name of a social worker over in Jobos who worked with the teenagers. They suggested he might be able to give me some information, so off I headed, backtracking to Jobos. I was worried to death about the welfare of Smokie, who by now probably had been without water or food, was possibly injured, and certainly would have put up a fight and somehow been disposed of. When I finally tracked down the social worker, making my way around the unfamiliar hamlet, it was nearly six o'clock in the afternoon. The fellow was very compassionate as he listened calmly to my, by now, tearfully stammering explanation of the circumstances. When I had finished the part about the apparent tracks of two horses coming up from the beach, he stopped me and gently told me to follow him to a nearby street because he had an idea of who might be involved. We stopped in front of a ramshackle small house where he told me to wait outside by my car as he knocked on the door. It was opened by a frail old woman who greeted him warmly and invited him in. The wait seemed interminable for me. Fay was standing by my side when the front door opened and the man walked out. He was holding the end of a pillowcase I recognized as mine, with the weight of an object at the bottom. The pillowcase was very still, and I let out a cry of grief as he handed it gently to me and said how sorry he was. I wailed, "Oh Smokie. My poor, dear Smokie." I opened up the pillowcase to take a look at the body, and a barely audible, croaking voice said, "Bonjour, bonjour." Crying even more now, I tenderly lifted Smokie out of the pillowcase and folded her softly into my arms. I asked the fellow to get some tap water from the house, and I let Smokie lick it from my fingers. By now, the old woman had come out to see the happy commotion and explained the situation.

Apparently, her grandson lived with her and had already been in trouble with the police. He'd come home before noon that day, and without explaining anything to the grandmother, had brought several pillowcases into the house, and left them in his room. He left quickly and had not returned. For a few hours she could hear men's voices coming from his room and occasionally some barking dogs but was too frightened to investigate. Then there was silence for the rest of the afternoon. When the social worker had come to the house to inquire, she led him to the room, where he went in, saw the pillowcases, and grabbed the greasy one, according to what I had related about the circumstances in my house that morning. Without opening it, thinking it was, by now, the dead parrot, he had gently handed it to me, expressing his sorrow.

What a surprise to everyone. What a delight to me and to Fay. The social worker suggested that I change Smokie's name to Lazarus.

He went back into the house where he retrieved the other two pillowcases, which contained a 35mm camera, some nautical items, and two large, beautiful seashells, one a Queen Conch and the other a King Conch, or Spanish Helmet shell. That seemed ironic to me, Jobos being a fishing port community, but I guessed the child had never owned such pretty things. It certainly was not a lucrative robbery for them because we had never owned a television or a phone, and I had no interest in jewelry, fine china, or fancy clothes. They might just have gone to the trouble of capturing the parrot out of spite. I thanked the social worker and the grandmother and drove home jubilantly, with Smokie nestled in my lap. I did not wash off the grease because African Gray parrots preen themselves with a chalky powder that comes from a gland on their backs. I knew the gentle rain would clean her in her outdoor cage. She stayed put there for a few days, seemingly none the worse for the wear and talking up a storm, repeating her way through every assortment of her routines..

I had twice relented in pursuing a divorce, and Albert and I still both lived in the house in a modicum of convenience and peace. When he came home that night, Al was furious at the incident. He went down to the police station the next morning to press charges. He eventually backed down when the families of the two teenagers responsible for the intrusion agreed to send each of the boys to family members in the States where there would be more discipline and monitoring for at least a year. I did not care about any of the items or the ultimate resolution. I was just so thankful to have Smokie, my indomitable companion, back home and safe.

Reflections and Loose Ends

That is a mostly bare-bones account of how I sleep-walked my way through most of my fourteen year stint in Puerto Rico. I enjoyed incredible adventures, but yielded what little integrity I felt I had, in the reflected shadow of Albert Emerson Slaughter, my larger-than-life mate and fellow miscreant. He had a great sense of humor and an endless stash of amusing incidents and observations. As a spouse Al tacitly afforded me total freedom to pursue whatever whims and projects I wished, whether daily or long-term. Like me, he loved to sing and dance, and he soulfully played the harmonica, breathing and spitting his way through country western, Latino tunes, international favorites, and even classical melodies. However, the tunes, like his old jokes, had begun to grate on me.

Generous with his time and money, (and not infrequently with that of others) he especially went to great lengths to entertain friends and relatives who would come down to live with us and wait out the cold winters of the north. But it was becoming increasingly too easy for me to turn a blind eye to Al's propensity to appropriate the unguarded property of others or to cook up shady deals.

Just as in my carefree childhood of shoplifting and scheming I now, like Al, functioned easily in the gray areas of moral turpitude. I will not guess from where his facility sprang. But I know that my daily shape-shifting from a camouflaged approval seeking to an impudent, confrontational comraderie, to a determined harshness came from a resentment of what I falsely interpreted as my father's obsequious behavior in public. I knew I had been attracted to Albert in reaction to that. I disregarded the feelings of others and with moral blinders, focused only on my momentary target or plan. I had sought the company of those whom I presumed held the key to my safety, security, or receiving of love. I was arrogantly dismissive of anyone I deemed did not figure into that equation. Thus, perhaps not in sex but definitely in manipulation of reality, Albert and I made good bedfellows. On that chord, although Albert was always affectionate to me our sex life had never satisfied either of us. It was now a faded memory. So, after a particularly harrowing incident when Albert, drunk and out-of-control, had mindlessly injured a neighbor's cow, I told him I that I was determined to follow through on yet a third attempt at divorce

I had grown increasingly attracted to my French friend, Violette, While Al went off in the barrio each day, who knows where, Violette and I had become lovers. We managed to have trysts at her home or in a hotel in San Juan. I even had boldly approached her husband, Sidney, to warn him I was proposing to Violette that we both get divorced and move in together in another part of Puerto Rico. He smirked and wished me luck.

As was sung to a little boy … life is what happens when you're busy making other plans …

**Two photos with Nan and child Fay, with a dead moray eel;
third photo is Fay in striped shirt on deck in front of sea;**

Any Port in a Storm

In June that year, my mother asked me to book a flight from Puerto Rico to Fort Lauderdale so I could drive her up to Long Island where she stayed for the summer in Southold. Once again placing Smokie with my friend, Violette, to be cared for while I was absent, I flew up with Fay in tow. One thing led to another, and I made the decision to begin life anew on the South Fork of Long Island. Virginia Fay would soon be five years old and I needed to commit to living where she could continue her education uninterrupted. Puerto Rico was fast becoming a dead end for me, since neither Albert nor I wanted to give up the simple but spacious house we had built ourselves in front of the Caribbean. I had lived in the barrio seven years, with so many memorable experiences, horrendous, comical, and poignant. Yet I recognized that it was time to regroup elsewhere.

In a weekend excursion to a gay bar in East Hampton I had met a woman who ran a guest house in Sag Harbor. She invited me to stay at her place free of charge until I could establish myself. I went back to Pozuelos to pack, leaving behind fourteen years of memories. I shipped up my truck on a container ship with four packing boxes filled with beachcombing "treasures," a few good books and 78-speed records of opera and country music (go figure?!), some of Fay's toys and clothes, and the parrot's sturdy indoor cage. Smokie herself came with me in a cat carrier on my lap, relatively quiet, but still occasionally entertaining the other passengers with some of her multilingual performances during the three-hour flight.

The bird quickly adapted to her new surroundings, enduring a nine-month long stint in a closed-in house but occasionally permitted to explore the many tiny rooms. I then allowed myself to be blackmailed by my mother into a return to teaching, when she insisted on that before she would loan me the down payment for a house. In retrospect, I actually bless her now, as I enjoy the pension of a civil servant, but at the time, I bristled at the "imposition."

In May of 1985, Virginia Fay, Smokie, and I moved into our own home in the "service-provider," blue collar section of Southampton. It did not seem to have a proper right angle in its construction, with no cellar, just a crawl space. Over the years since its origin as a beach cottage in 1926, it had had three different sources of heat installed. At present there was no heat except for one room with an electric blower in the wall. But the mortgage was in my name, and I would navigate life's waters in this ship, and face the storms as they came.

Observations

The above vignettes and the few that follow below are highlights that stood out to me as I had begun a self-inquiry into my lifelong patterns. Most of the incidents horrified me as I saw my depravity and moral turpitude. Some vignettes illustrate the moments of light-hearted adventure and interaction I experienced. They attempt to provide a window into how I had passively lived my life through other's larger-than-life personalities. First I took on Albert's energies and outlook, enjoying what I tasted but never seeing or savoring the fruits of my own inner beauty. And I would eventually immerse myself in the lifestyle of another flamboyant personality, an actress/singer in Manhattan. The mystery of power within myself was still invisible to me.

This is my cautionary tale. It is in print to share the lessons I learned. Like the parable's younger son, I followed my heart, grabbed at all that life offered, but did not know or honor self or others. I had not as yet descended deeply enough into my self-made hell to feel the empty desperation.

I returned to New York and spent over two decades in the Hamptons. The first two years I did garden maintenance, housecleaning jobs, and home nursing care. Then, a fluency in Spanish assured a Title Seven graduate degree in Bilingual Special Education from Adelphi University, and ironically, almost twenty years once more, as a classroom teacher. Motherhood though, had graciously softened me and I did not bring confusion and pain into the educational arena.

As a woman who loves sex with guys but finds deeper emotional fulfillment with women lovers, I yet again latched onto a larger-than-life person. I continued my pattern of approval seeking though, and lived much of my life through her. She was a loyal, good humored woman, an independently wealthy professional entertainer who lived in a doorman building in Greenwich Village. But she was prone to depression and emotional outbursts, and thus a high-maintenance partner. I spent twenty-three years in a tumultuous, on again-off again, week-ends and summers relationship.

Although both of us were bisexual, our liaison demanded a bi-coastal stamina because she lived full time in Manhattan and I in Southampton. Week-ends, when we couldn't golf, I traveled into Manhattan, and she spent summers at my house in the "service provider," less-than-POSH, section of Southampton on Noyac Road. On her nickel, we enjoyed first class, world-wide travel during school vacations, when my daughter either went to camp or to Puerto Rico to be with Albert, and his sister, who had moved there next door to him.

Part of the problem within this relationship was due to the guilt I felt about placing so much time and energy into my lover rather than my daughter. Virginia Fay already had handled so much emotional turmoil in her young life, with an equanimity far beyond her years. I believe she actually was, from a very young age, the wisest and most emotionally developed of all of us. To her credit, and my great relief, she found solace in academic excellence. At her own insistence, she skipped junior year in Southampton High School and still became co-valedictorian of her graduating class. Then she went on to graduate Phi Beta Kappa and summa cum laude from Wellesley College in Wellesley, MA.

With her innate wisdom and maturity of spirit, Virginia asked both Albert and me to walk her down the aisle when she married her first love, Donald. She even asked my partner to be in the wedding party also. Five years later, I began to find my real self, broke off the "twenty-two-years-too-long" relationship and sought refuge in the bosom of family, being a live-in "Nana" to my newborn granddaughter, Audrey, in Rhode Island. This is where the inner child emerged and now flourishes, laughing innocently and freely.

Until that occurred however, there are a few more vignettes to illustrate how I still was learning mastery within the illusion of fear-based, shadowed energies. The scenes depict a compromised, splintered woman, still vindictively judging others for her own choices.

Chapter Fourteen

Suffering's Vortex Moves North

1985 and 1986 – Southampton, NY

A Pal Betrayed

It was a tough first winter for the two of us and Smokie, as the palette of summer colors turned to ambers and beige. The walks down to the beach through the wooded paths and soggy swamp reeds became wonderlands of damp, blown-about leaves. But the sand was uninviting, the water impenetrable, and the blustering wind seemed to whine as much as my heart. Fay could not understand the cold beach. Her life of five years had centered on a warm, come-hither beachfront enveloping her in multiple daily walks and spontaneous plunges into the sub-tropical waters. It became a descent into depression and near punishment to visit the beach now. I later grew to appreciate the stark beauty of the winter beachfront landscape but that winter in the house took a demanding toll on our energy.

The three of us found refuge from the numbingly damp cold by hunkering down in Virginia Fay's bedroom, the only room with heat. The darkness came on so early, and quickly plunged us into a long restless night. Smokie fared no better. We had no other animals at the time so she was alone much of the day. She sang and talked less when we arrived home and developed a pulmonary condition that the vet said seemed part physical, but mostly emotional. It was a long season for us, but as all things cyclical, winter doldrums gradually eased into longer daylight hours and the glorious welcome of pastel. The pinks, yellows, whites, and violets of the spring flowers seemed determined to cheer us up.

We spent as much time as possible outside, as spring led to summer's leafy green fullness and Smokie eventually was allowed to navigate the back yard trees. I took a chance on this. I knew it would be only a matter of time before she flew off to investigate her new neighborhood, literally from a bird's eye view. But I understood and honored her avian urge. She had been captured and denied her natural jungle habitat, and I felt for her. She would always come down from the trees to my shoulder when I called her. She knew where her food source was, or so it seemed to me.

Then one afternoon she did not call down to me, to let me know her whereabouts. She did not return for supper and I grew concerned. I had seen red-tailed hawks in the neighborhood, and knew how flocks of crows could gang up on other birds. I drove around the area for a few miles in each direction, and down to the beachfront. No sign or sound of Smokie. So we went sadly, but hopefully to bed that night. At least it was warm in summertime and there were no storms predicted. The next morning I drove around the neighborhood, posting signs on telephone poles and at the local delicatessens and coffee shops. I even went into town and posted them at the banks and supermarkets. We knocked on doors inquiring about any sightings, and then drove around calling her name each day. But three days went by with no results.

On the afternoon of the fourth day, a woman called the house and asked if I owned a gray parrot with a bright red tail. I feared bad news about feathers or a body being discovered, "Well," she said, "there's a bird like that that's been hanging around my chicken coop, eating all the hens' corn and making a fuss about not sharing the greens and vegetable scraps I toss down in the yard."

"Yep, that's Smokie alright," I joyously sang. "Where do you live?"

"That's what's so strange," said the woman. I live in front of the beach and the chicken coop is practically in the sand, just a bit higher up from the storm surge line. I wouldn't think a parrot would be hanging around a beach, so I didn't believe my eyes, at first. Then it started to talk all these different languages, and I knew it was a parrot!"

I breathed a long, relieved sigh.

"I was telling my friend about it on the phone and she said that she'd seen a poster in the store about it, describing the colors and everything. She gave me your name and phone number, so here I am, calling."

I practically screamed, "What's your street, leading down to the beach? Describe your house and I'll be right over. Thank you so, so much. You don't know how happy you've made me." I cried all the way over on the less than five minute ride. Fay calmly, happily soothed me by chirping, "Mommy, I knew Smokie was alright. You always say she's our pal. I knew she was okay, Mommy."

At the woman's beachfront house, I stopped the car and Fay and I got out. I could see the chicken coop and fenced in area. It was obvious who was ruling the roost, as a flurry of light and dark gray feathers with a glimpse of a long red tail bopped and flitted among the furiously clucking hens. I whistled to Smokie and everything came to a standstill. She fluttered up to the top of the coop, called out, "Bonjour, bonjour. Comment ça va," and made an immediate beeline over to my shoulder, landing with a breathless, "Je suis arrivée."

"Golly," called out the woman, ambling over to the car, "I wish I had that on camcorder!"

I thanked her profusely and asked her if she wanted any compensation for the feed that Smokie had probably eaten, and perhaps the slowdown of egg production from the parrot's interference with the hens' routine. She declined, saying that the whole thing had been so amusing and that she never knew a parrot could talk so intelligibly and say so many things. She mentioned that there were times when she actually thought there were Spanish-speaking men outside and huge barking dogs. She found the whole episode quite entertaining. We thanked each other again, Smokie stayed on my shoulder as I got into the car, then she hopped down to snuggle in my lap on the short ride home. It was a very happy conclusion of the day. That is, for Fay and myself. I am sure that Smokie found the ensuing period of house arrest a bit stultifying. I resolved to be a more careful steward of her welfare, grateful for the woman's kindness, but a bit less trusting of Smokie's safety outside the house.

It had occurred to me that yes, she had known how to make her way back to our beachfront home in Puerto Rico, because it was directly in front of the beach. It was also up on pilings and the surrounding trees were mostly coconut palms. It was distinguishable as her home territory. Not so for the house in Southampton. It was a smaller, one story home, set back two blocks from the beach, with taller oak trees forming a canopy. Smokie probably flew comfortably toward the beach, as she always had, but the return to home was obscured and unfamiliar.

This buried awareness had dimly glimmered in my self-absorbed psyche before I had even allowed Smokie to venture freely into our yard. But I had avoided looking at it consciously and had been remiss in protecting her from the real circumstances. When she was missing for those almost four days, I had finally allowed the awareness to surface and be examined. I felt chagrined that I had not been a better shepherd to my "flock" of one, but a small part of me still argued for freedom over caution.

The question of Smokie's freedom over caged existence soon became merely academic. This new relationship was again setting off alarm bells within me. I had cavalierly ignored the cautionary inner voice when I had mismanaged my beginning relationship with Albert fourteen years before. I again disregarded the unease and strain that I was increasingly experiencing when Dinah stayed at our house. Although she enjoyed Smokie's antics and loyalty, Dinah grew more critical of what she considered the "noise" created by a talented parrot. However, I was quite immersed in the energies of sexual freedom and the exhilarating city-life opportunities offered by Dinah's newly established presence in my life. I offered little resistance to her complaints.

With full acknowledgment to myself that I was betraying a dear friend and companion, I failed to stand up for Smokie. I refused to examine the rawness of the wound I was inflicting on myself and daughter, and on this indomitable creature whom I loved dearly and who had given me and Virginia Fay such pleasure and love in return for a bit of stewardship. I allowed my need for approval and comfort to rule over my goodness of heart. I told myself that it was really best for the parrot because of the lonely days approaching when I would go back to work again in the Fall. I arranged to put her on consignment in a pet shop in Port Jefferson which specialized in birds. Smokie was sold rapidly to a couple in Sayville, who ironically had the same last name as mine.

Once I walked out of that pet store, leaving behind a part of my heart and my own sense of integrity, I never saw Smokie again. My soul had presented me an opportunity to confront and transmute the energies of anxiety and self protection which I had taken on in my choice of birth circumstances. But I had yet again sold my soul to another person's influence. I drove home ignoring both my heart and my young daughter's pleas of, "Why, Mommy, why?"

African Gray parrot
(Sketch by Gisela Brogi)

April 1999 - High School in the Hamptons

With a Troubled Teddy Bear

"Listen, Hank," I murmured, as several 10th graders ambled by. "I haven't got a clue what your situation is, but from what you just said, it sounds like you should get a lawyer."

"That's just what somebody else told me," he whined, trying to talk in a whisper.

How many colleagues' shoulders has this poor guy dampened today? Actually, how can this conversation be happening, when all I'm trying to do is make a reservation in the computer lab for my 3rd period class tomorrow?

I had seen Hank there with his English Lit. class and asked about his new baby. I felt a pang of nostalgia, remembering how fast Virginia Fay had grown up on me. Now I'm being force-fed how his wife throws him out to sleep elsewhere and is turning the kids against him. I'm wondering how Hank, galumphy and rumpled like a kid's teddy bear, soft-spoken and gentle, could ever have offended anyone enough to have them throw plastic dishes at his head.

So, as the kids at their computers, begin to tune in, realizing we're not talking about world events, but actually have lives outside of this high school, I start to inch my way into the hallway, with Hank in earnest pursuit.

"Hank, do you need a place to stay tonight? My daughter's away at college and you could use her room. Just know that there's not a right angle in the house and you'll have to plow your way through a week's accumulation of debris, but you're certainly welcome. I live in Southampton, on Noyac Road."

"Oh, wow, that's really nice of you, Nan," he emotes, "But I'm tutoring here after school and then I have to do some home tutoring out in Montauk. I wouldn't even get to Noyac Road until after nine o'clock."

No wonder this guy's wife is nuts. When's the last time he's gotten it up? Considering he lives in Speonk, he must be catatonic when he gets home. Oh, well there're always two sides.

Now that I've gone this far, I can't back out on the guy, so I tell him there's no problem what time he gets there, because I'll leave the sliding door open on the deck, and the back light on, and that I'll be up anyway. Which is a lie because I'm usually zonked by eight-thirty or nine, but what the heck, I think back to my divorce scenarios with Albert and how we could have used a demilitarized zone of sorts.

This idle thought propels me to urge him again to get a lawyer.

"Look, Hank, like I said, emotions run so high in marriage difficulties, and if you are thinking about a divorce, you've got to have the advice of a lawyer, someone who's not personally involved and can give you objective advice. And keep a log of incidents and dates, and what might have precipitated them."

"Sounds like you've been through this," he says sheepishly.

By now the bell has rung and I've effectively lost my prep time, so I figure, what the heck.

"You couldn't imagine how things can escalate," I explain. "I mean, by now ... let's see, that was probably back around '81, so, yeah, after eighteen years I can actually see the humor in it, but at the time it was scary. But anyway, I had my own American Civil War. Albert played Confederate and I was Union. I think at times our insidious sabotage tactics resembled some of those battles." We're walking down the hall by now, so I launch into the gory details of one of my more memorable divorce incidents.

"Hank, I'm telling you, things can happen. My husband and I ... this is when I lived in Puerto Rico ..."

"You lived in Puerto Rico? I didn't know that!"

"Yeah, fourteen years, from nineteen seventy to eighty four. Anyway ..."

"How'd you get to PR?"

"I went down there as a nun, but then I met Albert, and after we spent Christmas in a lighthouse, I sort of got invited to leave the nunnery ... so after I got drummed out, so to speak, I went back down and lived with Al."

"Wait a minute ... what's this about you being a nun?"

"Yes, for nearly ten years."

He whispers then, as if the walls could hear, "... and you're not saying you slept with this guy ... in a lighthouse ... at Christmas?!"

"Yes, Hank," I gently urge him to keep walking as I say, "this is ancient history now."

Then I quickly continue, "Hank, let me finish the divorce stuff. I mean, it's funny now, after all these years, and it'll help you not to panic when things seem to get a bit hyper ... and they will ... with you and your wife."

How could this guy ever panic? He's in perpetual slow-mo. Oh well.

So, as we walk along the hall, I launch into the gory details of how Albert went up onto the roof of the house one day, and shouted down to me, asking if I still wanted the divorce.

"After I had called back up to him from inside the house, that yes, I did, still want the divorce, is when the chain saw started its whine from somewhere up on the roof. It wasn't until the chain saw blade came poking through the ceiling that I began to get the drift. I stood there watching a not-measured-at-all rectangular opening roughly carved out of the roof. Albert called down to me through the opening, 'Is this where you always wanted that skylight?'"

'Al,' I said, 'this is ridiculous. Come on down from there.'

'No it isn't, honey,' he said peering through the hole. 'I'm going to make a couple of them. Where do you want the others?'

'Al, come on. This is scaring the baby,' I said to him through the unexpected skylight.

"Anyway, I took our three year - old and drove into town in the truck to do some chores. I figured I'd eliminate the audience, you know, and the 'joke' would fall flat. When I came back two hours later, there were two more unmatched skylights, plus a side door leading out to a twelve-foot drop, and no more front stairs. You know how some houses are built on telephone pole pilings? Well, ours was at least twelve feet high so the hurricane tides could wash underneath if needed. So there I was looking up and wondering how I was going to get into the house, or even if I should go back in. I mean, things were ominously quiet."

"Well, about five minutes later, Al came back without the chain saw, thank god, and told me remorsefully, not to worry. He said he'd rig a stairway of sorts, for now and would build a new one the next day, and that he'd repair the holes in the roof and the side wall."

"'Before it rains, I hope,' is all I said. And that was that."

"Wow, weren't you scared?" Hank inquired.

"No, not really. I knew enough to leave and let him get his anger and frustration out of his system. I was his fifth wife, Hank, so it's not like he hadn't been through divorce before. I guess he was as angry at himself as he was at me … or life, or whatever. But it wasn't like he was ever physically abusive. It was more psychological and emotional. We laughed about it the next day. That was one thing that had always carried us through hard times. We both had a sense of humor and could appreciate the farcical moment."

"But what I'm trying to tell you, Hank, is that in marriage troubles, things can get explosive. Humor can save the day – or save lives!"

November 1999

Thanksgiving and Road Kill

In 1989, Fay had chosen to be addressed by her first name, Virginia. Even though I and all her friends from elementary school knew her as Fay, she made sure that the teachers in her Intermediate school would see her listed as Virginia. It took me about a year to make the transition. At first I was delighted because I had always wanted to call her Ginger anyway. But she promptly demolished that attempt when she constantly reinforced that it was, "Virginia, Mom, not Ginger, not Snap, not Westy, just VIRGINIA."

So I'm driving myself and Virginia to Thanksgiving dinner at my sister Ginny's in Southold. Drinks at three, dinner at four. These are the orders. Ginny is the family matriarch now. It just worked out that way, and their house can hold the massive group that seems to materialize each year. There'll be thirty seven today, give or take a few tag-a-longs. Friends and family are always welcome to savor G&R's generous larder. So we all capitulate to the one rule and have a marvelous time: jackets and ties for the guys, whatever age they are, and comfortable dress-up for the gals.

Today I chose to drive around the crook that is Riverhead, between the South Fork where we live, and Southold on the North Fork. This is harder on the mileage, but is mindless driving as opposed to the aggravation and cost of the two ferries, by way of Shelter Island. We got near Aquebogue when Virginia noticed the throw-away camera in the center floorboard holder.

"So what's with the camera, Mom?"

"A project I'm developing."

"Oh?"

Next thing you know, we're hysterically laughing, squealing, actually. It's always been so much fun with my daughter. She deals with her nutcase of a mother because somehow, thank goodness, she can see the humor in the oddity of my pursuits.

She will have reached her twenty first birthday in exactly a month, this being November 25 and Virginia the product of a "virgin birth" of sorts, being born on Christmas Day. She revels in the skewed and unconventional life I've led. It gives her fodder for one-upmanship with her friends at Wellesley College when they're telling stories about their parents.

Now that she's acquired a bona fide boyfriend of late, she's really got a stash of aces up her sleeve to keep him guessing about her gene pool. She can draw from my being one of forty cousins, then my convent stories interspersed with accounts of my lesbian lifestyle. Weave into that mixture her father, Albert E. Slaughter, thirty-nine years living in Puerto Rico, by way of good ol' boy, southern Baptist Roanoke Rapids, NC, and a WWII stint as a Navy hard-hat diver in the Pacific. Virginia can keep them all rolling in the aisles.

Anyway, we're squealing merrily because I explained that the camera is for the road kill.

Virginia is trying to gasp out the words between fits of choking laughter.

"Mom, who is going to buy a book about *road kill*?"

"Well I do think those who can appreciate the irony will buy it. Of course it's not exactly going to be a coffee table book, and I'll give the proceeds to the Hamptons Wildlife and Rehabilitation Center. I'm going to call it *A Stretch of Country Road*.

"It seems ironic, doesn't it, that the folks who come out to the Hamptons to get away from the hectic bustle of the city and enjoy the scenery and the wildlife here, are the very same people who are cutting down huge swathes of woods and erecting massive trophy homes? This just displaces the foxes and raccoons and whatever other wild creatures, which are then forced to find other shelter and food and wind up crossing the back roads and being run down by the same folks who are zooming their way to the week-end *country* retreats."

"Anyway, I got the idea when I saw the body of a muskrat across from the Coast Grill on Noyac Road. It must have been headed for the pond from the inlet. Its coat was such a beautiful, sleek reddish brown and I really wanted to see its webbed feet. I happened to have the camera in the car from one of those frou-frou courses I'm taking where I have to photograph posters that we make in cooperative groups.

"So I stopped the car and took a picture of this beautiful creature. Then I started thinking about all the squashed animals I see on my way to and from school each day, and how ironic it is that we're forcing them into the roads just to survive. I see more road kill in two weeks here on a three-mile stretch of Noyac Road than I do in an entire summer up in Maine.

"The animals have nowhere else to go, Virginia. We fence off every little parcel and prevent them from getting to the water they need or from finding mates or food. It's like we're killing the goose that laid the golden egg.

"Hence, the photo project! Besides the muskrat, I've got a possum, two deer, a raccoon, and a baby fox. I could have gotten a whole family of raccoons, but before I could walk back to get the picture, a pick-up truck had flattened two of them. I don't want the photos to be too gruesome. Just make a statement. The fox was right across from Noyac Golf Club, in front of the sign for Morton Wildlife Preserve. If that isn't irony, what is?"

The levity had given way to my preaching, so the laughter was gone. But Virginia still laid her head on my shoulder, like she does when she needs to let me know that no matter how off the wall I may seem sometimes, she still loves me and secretly admires the obvious, yet somehow endearing imbalance.

Southampton, NY - March 2000

Shift Happens

Why is it that you're all over me in bed, whenever I just need to curl up and go to sleep? That's when you insist on plopping on top of me. And now, when I desperately need you, you're trying to push away from me. Pleeeeease, I just need a warm body to hug close! Please, Cannoli!

I'm doubled over, grabbing at the washing machine with its piles of dirty laundry, sobbing. Not crying, sobbing. Almost like that time I got the call about Mom's death and I slowly crumpled onto the steps near the kitchen, and let out those long, interminable sobs. Then, as now, they seemed to come from the bowels of the earth and up through my own entrails. They didn't seem to need any intake of breath, just a wailing outflow rasping against my vocal cords, until I was empty. And then I'd wrack in some more air and let it out in a steady, punching stream of guttural sounds. That kind of sobbing.

Oh my god, where is this coming from? Just let me hold you. I need you, well, not really you, but your comfort. I mean, cats are supposed to be intuitive, right? You're supposed to feel my pain, Cannoli. Where's Spicey, anyway? She was born in a barn. She knows what it's like to be afraid, to be at a dead end, or a fork in the road, and not know which way to turn. She'd be sensitive enough not to strain away from me.

Damn it, Cannoli! Okay then, go. You're no help anyway. You've never known anguish and fear. Born in Samantha-somebody's bed, always cuddled and held 'til Virginia and I took you home here. God, why don't I still have my dogs! Oh, Blackjack; poor Warlock, forgive me, I'm so sorry.

This is streaming through my mind as my soul is seared with a sudden bolt of insight that leaves me weak-kneed, sobbing in the laundry room, anguished and guilty for those years that I now see as wasteful, lost. One minute I'm doing mundane chores; the next I'm sideswiped by a roaring locomotive of consciousness. The insight I experience now is like the oyster's grain of sand that festers in its nacre until the pearl is formed. In essence, it is an irritant and a bothersome intruder. It's been forcing itself into my very innards and becoming who I am. But under all my resistance it is still a feared object, even wrapped as the luster-coated pearl in my subconscious.

Is this what I've really been angry about all these years and could not voice? Am I ever going to face this and tell Dinah the truth? Just blurt out that resentment is the painful nugget, the kernel around which things are festering in my soul? I must tell her. I know I have been too cowardly to call her on her self-absorption, too afraid of losing her. So the end result is that I've allowed my daughter to shoulder the consequences of Dinah's need for constant reassurance and my need to continually placate her.

It's now painfully clear to me that acrimonious dissatisfaction is eating me up inside and the anger I feel towards Dinah just comes out as physical ailments in myself. Yet in all those sessions together, at Dinah's insistence, with her shrink, Dr. Amirzadeh, I was still too cowardly to voice my soul's longing. I refused to admit that I want to spend more time with my daughter. The bottom line is that I can bear only limited time with Dinah herself.

Well, how could I reveal something to her that I'd spent our entire relationship refusing to acknowledge even to myself? It's probably because I am at this crossroads now, what with Virginia graduating from Wellesley in two months, and the house up for sale, and me talking openly in the faculty room at East Hampton about retiring, and not being all that discrete about who or what gender, my "pal" really is. All of these factors are probably jiggling these memories and juxtaposing them into some gorgeously kaleidoscopic monster of insight.

Damn, I am wacked out. I can truly *see* what has been at the very heart of my soul's unrest. I recall miserably now, how I had come up here to Southampton from Puerto Rico with five-year-old Virginia Fay. I'd pictured long, lazy summers in a canoe with my daughter, showing her the nesting sites of swans and ducks, or on Little Fresh Pond, scouting out the ospreys, watching tadpoles develop, and tracking the snapping turtles on their way to lay eggs.

Where did that all go? How could I have been so weak and unfocused to have sacrificed that for a glitzy, bohéme, yet shadowed lifestyle I thought was real? And then I tried unsuccessfully to sustain these juxtaposed lifestyles? For a lover rich enough to buy us into Noyac Golf Club at sixty grand a piece, yet so needy and self-centered that I had to be with her at almost every weekend moment, and therefore, not present to my daughter and her legitimate childhood needs. Now I see it. *I* was the fragile one. *I* bent to Dinah's every whim, ministered to each of her "crises." Yet it was my young daughter who bore the brunt of the emotional weight thrust onto her.

Yes, okay, Dinah did buy that inflatable plastic boat, and we did use it on the pond. But it had to always be the three of us - God forbid, Dinah should spend an hour or so alone. And the conversation would inevitably drift to golf, so Fay would be out of the loop and need to amuse herself in the boat. Like any six, seven, or eight-year-old, she would vie for our attention, by interrupting. It wasn't obvious to Dinah that she herself was hogging the "quality time" with conversation about a subject Fay could care less about, or hated actually. Golf was what had kept me away from her for five hours earlier in that day. Then when we would finally come home to Fay to do some fun family things, Dinah would want to rehash every stroke of the morning's round.

Finally, not able to take the strain of trying to listen to both of them, I would tell Dinah that this was Fay's time now, and attempt to engage them both in scouting for birds and turtles. This inevitably resulted in Dinah's sulking and my finally blowing up. Virginia Fay, more stable and mature than either of us, dealt with it and always picked up the pieces.

Oh, my darling, darling child, my Ginger Snap! I am so sorry ... and the sobbing starts again.

But the insight has other levels. I now feel it, as I sob. I recognize the pall of anxiety invading my spirit, that feeling of being orphaned when my mother died. It is the self-same orphaning I sensed but refused to look at, as I swaggered through an angry childhood. Unguided and at loose ends, I was piqued at my parents for their merrily *laissez faire* approach to child-rearing and hated my own fragility for not ever voicing my confusion and need. Yet I chose to embody those energies. I chose those birth circumstances and influences so that I could transcend the sadness. I have not done that yet, but my soul is certainly nudging me that way. At least now I am becoming aware of a pattern of blaming what is outside of me.

Here I am, doing the same thing with a partner. My vocal cords are frozen in the grip of fear. I'm frightened by the looming possibility that my honesty will cause me to lose Dinah's companionship. My anguish is further compounded by a lurking unease that the presence of Dinah in my life is not only insufficient, it is actually detrimental. Still, I feel I've made a trade-off and it's what I'm clinging to. I don't have a strong core of self, an inner strength lighting my way, shining from the depths of my known Truth. I don't know who I am, and Dinah is a familiar presence. I am beginning to recognize my life-long lack and how I've failed both daughter and lover, and within them, myself. And so, I cry again.

I feel such sadness that I, the other adult, didn't seize any of the many moments through the years, when irritation would well up, to just tell Dinah, "no." To say that Virginia is my child and I need, no, I *want* to enjoy her before she grows up and goes away, that she needs to know that she comes first. I would tell Fay this constantly, but I didn't live it. Only when Dinah wasn't around, and even then, the two of us "adults" would be on the phone, Dinah's neediness roping me in, even from Manhattan. My daughter, the real adult before her time, sat on the sidelines.

The layers of my own confusion had been peeled away somewhat, through the years, and I had several times skirted close to telling Dinah what was in my gut. But I never could really formulate it in such a way that the truth would not hurt her so much. That I actually *would* choose my daughter over her, if it came down to that.

Oh, God, that's it! Through all these fifteen years I could not get myself to admit it to her: I would choose Virginia over her!

And so, I failed them both. I truly lucked out that my child is such an old soul, that she could see into my fragility and instead of punishing me, she buoyed me up by her single-minded pursuit of academic excellence. She could so easily have crashed. So accessible were the drugs, the sex, and the myriad of distractions for teenagers in the Hamptons.

I had imploded in my own childhood. Yet she didn't. She saved herself and me. Here is Dinah, waiting in the wings for me to retire from my teaching job so that we can travel at any moment and not be inundated by crowds of families on school vacations. Yet I know I don't want to be with her uninterruptedly. I am bitter towards her narcissistic, "studied helplessness."

I am really going to have to spill my guts to her, and damn the consequences. God, am I really fifty six years old and only just now learning to be true to myself ... to others? But I know in my heart that even if I do break things off, as I have before, I'll still go back to her eventually. In my own convoluted manipulations of the truth, I know I'll still trade off the truth for the "good life."

At least I'm not still sobbing.

Oh good, Spicey, you're here! Come on over here, baby. Cannoli just doesn't get it, does she?

Spring 2002 – A High School in the Hamptons

A Voyeur's Window onto Sadness

Interesting twist with both young women lying nude on that steel grate table, one on her back, the other face down on top of her. The one on her back must have been a bit uncomfortable. Well, being on her back was okay, but even with her knees bent over the side of the table, her feet didn't reach the floor. She had no way to brace herself when the one lying on top of her reacted to the whip. Must have been jarring. And jeez, could the one on top really have been enjoying it? Even with the pleasure of having her face snuggled into the ample breasts of the gal under her she still had to endure the fact that her bare buttocks were shining up to the dominatrix, and to anyone else in that barroom. What an exhibitionist! I guess that's what the S&M scene is, humiliation and pain. Whoa, primal stuff! I don't know why I let Dinah drag me along to this! Probably because deep down it fascinates me. Who's doing the suffering here?

Neat too, the way anyone could approach from any angle and observe up close. Well, as much as the dim lights and cigarette smoke would allow. And as long as it didn't interfere with the arc of that dom's swing. I wouldn't have wanted to get tangled in that! Boy, she knew how to use a whip. Not to mention whatever it took to squeeze into that red latex!

There wasn't much room to get close, but from the look of the welts on that kid's bottom, the dominatrix knew her whips, and whatever else was in that weird assortment of straps and paddles. Strange, how with each thwack or thump, that "victim" squealed with delight … didn't seem manufactured either. That must have been her thing, and she sure was getting off on it. Even when they paused to exchange the young woman underneath, nobody seemed to miss a beat. Wow, that was lame!

Anyway, that plump, young submissive kid sure had a comforting variety of bosoms to emote on. Boy, what a psychologist's "candy store" in that whole scene! Jarred me, though, made me queasy. Didn't even want to go, but as usual, I allowed myself to indulge Dinah's whimsy.

"So you're saying that María is absent today because she's at the hospital now with Maribel?" The principal's tinny, Mr.-Burns-from-the-Simpson's voice jogged me back to his office here in the high school.

God, had I been thinking out loud?

It seemed surreal to be sitting here early on a Monday morning, in a high school office in the Hamptons discussing a suicide attempt by one of my immigrant students, when last night I had been a hundred miles west, in New York's meat packing district. It was "Women's Night" at *The Lure*, a bar that is used for the underground S&M scene.

I am so-o-o not here.

"No, sir. María Susana called me from her own home. She was going to get some sleep before she came into classes. Maribel had called her last night from the hospital, after she'd had her stomach pumped, and asked Maria Susana to come and stay with her there. So when María Susana left a while ago to go home and get some sleep, she called me here at the high school to tell me about it. She was very nervous that she might be betraying Maribel's confidence, but I told her she had done the correct thing and that we would seek some help for Maribel."

"Yes, good … so where is Alfonso right now? I think he should handle this."

He was referring to the bilingual social worker the district had finally hired after so many years of the TESOL department's pleadings. We folks in our department, the Teaching of English to Speakers of Other Languages, seemed to function as a school-within-a-school most of the time, anyway.

For god's sake, the high school is more than twenty percent Latino now. Don't they get it that we need a Latino social worker here in the high school full-time?

"I think he's at the elementary school today, I murmured, wanting to blurt out, '*because you guys just can't see the writing on the wall?*'

Among our TESOL personnel, we joke that there must be signs in the airports in Cuenca, Medellín, San José, and Mexico City saying what a great place the Hamptons is for raising kids. "Learn a labor-driven business like landscaping, construction, or house painting! Then when you've learned the ropes, start your own business with your 'conpa'es,' and undercut your gringo boss for the local jobs!" *Hey, didn't my own Galway and Kilkenny ancestors do the same thing in New York City in the 1800's?*

Even our immigrant women make fantastic money here in this town … cash on the barrel head, with their housecleaning businesses, learning how to undercut each other. It's amazing when you try to call home about any of the kids' school work, and the office records show a variety of cell phones, beepers, and home phones. Usually, you get *la abuela* on the home phone. *Thank goodness for my fourteen years in Puerto Rico; I can use the Spanish vernacular to cut through the nicety crap. I know that grandmothers rule the roost. Abuela knows very well how to deal with Juanito.*

The principal's voice cuts into my reverie, "What I don't understand is, where are the parents; why aren't they at the hospital with her, or in here, discussing this whole thing?" he whines to me, with the phone on his shoulder, waiting for someone at the elementary school to locate Alfonso.

"Well, Maribel is actually nineteen, and was living more with her boyfriend than at home," I said. Then I continued, trying not to sound too pedantic, "A lot of these teen-agers are virtual strangers to their parents. They're raised by grandparents or aunts back in Ecuador, Colombia, Costa Rica, or Mexico, while mom and dad are up here for five or six years, carving out a life, Then the children are sent for, one or two at a time, only by then they're not kids anymore, really. They're teen-agers. The parents expect them to fit right in, and it just doesn't work that way."

The folks at the elementary school can't seem to locate the social worker, Alfonso, so I continue, "That's not always the case. I mean, their families are usually so close-knit, but with Maribel, the mother returned to Ecuador. The kid wanted to come here to live with her father, who has remarried. It seems he's not thrilled by her being here. There's a lot of tension between Maribel and the new wife. And actually, with Maribel, it seems the light's a little dim in the attic, anyway. But this attempt of hers is really because of her own boyfriend's dumping her recently. At least that's what María Susana seems to think."

By now, Alfonso is on the phone, so the principal is telling him the story and urging him to get over to the hospital to see how he can help. When he finishes with Alfonso, he turns to me and says, "Okay, Nan. Well, you tell María she did the right thing. And thank you, too, for coming to me right away." He gives me a nod of dismissal.

I've got to give him credit. He really acted decisively.

"I'll call María Susana's house this afternoon," I say as I leave. "She really needs her sleep right now."

I also want to mention to him that when our Latino kids give us two names for their first name, they *really* want to be called just that: *María*

Susana. But I don't. After thirteen years in this district, I pick my battles judiciously.

So I walk back down the hall to the classroom where thirty one Spanish-speaking teenagers are waiting to find out what kind of geometry quiz they're having tomorrow in my bilingual math class..

It's only 8:20 on Monday morning. Nine hours ago, I was a voyeur at an S&M scene, watching exhibitionists willingly submitting to pain and indignity inflicted by their lovers or friends. Now I'm privy to an incident of self-inflicted violence springing from some secret, deeply felt pain. Both scenes are a primal scream unleashed to the universe. It echoes within me too, this self-imposed pain.

Reflection

Isn't hindsight delicious? We get to witness ourselves playing a part, acting out a drama … taking it all so seriously. As soul encourages, poses questions, nudges and suggests, we gradually begin to dwell within. We slowly become aware that there is more to life than action-reaction. We can make conscious choices to follow the heart. We can freely elect to uncover our natural joy and the rhythmic flow of individuated frequency of godliness within our common humanity.

But I did not prove to be a good listener to this Comforter Within. There were rumblings in my psyche, disturbances in my sense of personal integrity yet I still sold my soul to the receiving of approval from another. It took me four more years to wrest my soul from the grip I had handed over to another. For a total of twenty-three years in New York's Manhattan and the Hamptons I looked only at the things and experiences which reinforced the skewed image I had of myself. But I chose to ignore an eroding sense of wholeness and physical and mental wellbeing. I chose to ignore a growing seed of possibility that I had an inner voice of knowing. I craved and enjoyed what Dinah so generously shared of her inherited fortune. It had taken me twelve years to enact the same dynamics with Albert in various urban and rural settings in Puerto Rico. Gender did not matter to me. What seemed to matter was an opportunity to find safety and security outside of myself.

I am so grateful to each partner, the man named Albert, and the woman who calls herself Dinah, for the mutual growth we provided each other. My heart expands in wonder and gratitude for who they are in essence and for their choices to dance with me for a time. They are me. We are One in this human escapade called life and love.

2006 and 2007 – Manhattan

Light at the End of the Maze

After retiring from the Hamptons public school district, in June 2006, I went on a last international trip with Dinah. For twenty-two years she had been very generous with her inheritance, paying for me on multiple ski excursions to France and Switzerland, and to California, Idaho, New Mexico, Montana, Utah, and Colorado. We had golfed in Ireland and Spain, as well as at Torrey Pines and Pebble Beach, and various PGA courses. We had wept together at many of the major WWII concentration camps in Poland, Czechoslovakia, and Latvia, and imagined the desolation and anguish felt by inmates in the prisons-now-museums of Russia and in the United States. We were privileged to drive ourselves southward along France's coast from Dieppe to Normandy, to witness firsthand the invasion sites where British, Canadian, and American military personnel had struggled and died, and we had roamed the beaches and the burial areas, thanking and praying.

However, much of the time, we bickered. Intertwined with the sightseeing, dining, sailing, and motoring, whether in Sicily or Florence, Athens, Hydra, or Crete, Tokyo, Hiroshima, Takayama, or Bermuda, we spent countless hours and untold energy arguing. Usually, it centered around sex, or lack of it, according to Dinah. Although we had a varied, and I felt, satisfying, sex life, and both enjoyed the risqué and unconventional, Dinah wanted more of it. She quite loudly, with opera-trained voice and dramatic flair, painfully made it known to me and to most of the folks on the street, train car, or plane cabin, just how much she missed frequent sex. The wailing complaints usually involved detailed demands, much to my chagrin and to the amusement or annoyance of those around us.

After I retired, Dinah splurged on a late September two-week excursion with nine other people, all strangers, to retrace, by van, donkey cart, and camel, the silk route around the Taklimakan Desert in western China, towards Tajikistan. One day above the city of Kashgar, we were riding camels around the shore of Lake Karakul, a plateau lake in the foot of the Muztag Ata Mountain which is reputed to be "the father of glaciers." Dinah's camel slipped on a pile of wet dung and collapsed to one side, toppling Dinah and then rolling over on top of her. As it tried multiple times to right itself, the camel repeatedly pinned Dinah's leg, cracking a small bone in her ankle. Dinah, ever the trooper, valiantly continued on the three last days of the trip, and saw a doctor when we got back to Manhattan.

I stayed in Manhattan to help her, and attended classes at the Art Students League on 57th Street. As the months went by, I gradually realized that this relationship was at a dead end. Dinah was a wonderful partner and a loyal friend. She was generous and authentic with her laughter and intelligent seeking of knowledge and experience. As a lover she was caring, fun, and patient. She inspired me with her single-minded pursuit of a successful career in musical entertainment. And she shared with me her fortune as we explored the world of travel and international culture. But it was over. I was slowly discovering a sense of self. A seed of honest self-evaluating was taking root. I ended our relationship after a disastrous, scream-fest during a last ditch, one-sided salvage effort on a weekend trip to Provincetown. By then, I already had registered my car in Rhode Island and in November of 2007 was no longer a New York resident.

Throughout my life I had followed my heart. I never had a plan, but leapt at whatever opportunity popped up which seemed to offer safety or security, momentary approval, love, or mostly, adventure and fun. For thirty seven years I had lived life through relationships with two larger-than-life people. At opposite ends of the social, economic, and sexual spectrums, both partners willingly danced with me in my choice to hand over my persona to them. Shape-shifting to what I thought would please them I conformed with the image I presumed they expected of me. I blindly plodded or careened through extended years of self-obliteration mixed with heights and depths of physical, mental, and emotional adventures. Both partners taught me a vast array of worldly knowledge and imparted to me immeasurable delights through their complicated, sensitive, yet joyously upbeat personalities. But I did not loosen my grip on a need for their approval, even though they never actually sought to live that dominance. They were each strong enough to be authentically themselves. I was the imposter in each relationship. It was a trade-off I misperceived as the basis for a status quo absence of conflict. What it did was to plunge me into conflict with myself. I traded off an exterior façade of adventure, risk, and risqué for an internal landscape that was bedraggled and war torn with self-conflict. It took me considerably more time to see my beauty.

Something though was now stirring within me which I could no longer ignore. A glimmer of authenticity beckoned to me. A long-shadowed sense of personal integrity sought to be uncovered. Truth was emerging. Soul would no longer take, "Later," for an answer.

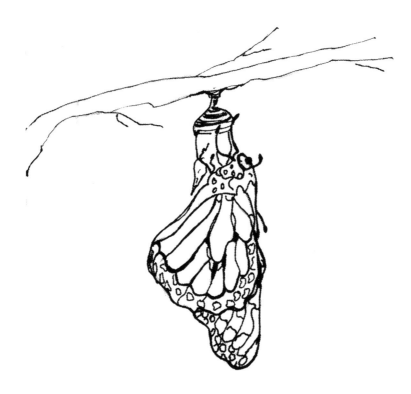

Butterfly Emerging from Chrysalis (Sketch by Gisels Brogi)

Reflection

I have been judgmental and arrogant for most of my life. I have been especially judgmental of myself. And therein lies the message I want to get across to whomever might persevere with me. In writing and praying this book, I was graced with moments of clarity and discernment. I peeled away layer upon layer of self protection until I saw how those defenses of judgment and arrogance had been erected.

I had continually played the tape of others' voices in my mind. Through whatever traumas I had chosen to experience in interaction with others from my infancy, through childhood and adolescence, and on into adulthood, I was listening to voices other than my own inner knowing. The tape had frozen in certain sections where a trauma had created static in my internal wiring and I reverted to that section as default. When I began to dampen the volume of those voices, and humbly gazed on my innate strength, I began to trust that I could actually choose to cut my dependence on those voices. I could with impunity, choose to look at those speakers as voicing whatever they themselves had embedded in their psyches from generations before them.

It is the human drama. It is actually a tragicomedy of errors. It is the cosmic joke we humans play on ourselves, conspiring together to create a world based on separation, otherness, and fear. I could regain a core personhood, not the exterior personality I had fashioned from fear. I felt, in every cell of my body, knew in every pulse of consciousness, that I was one with God, and thus one with everything in creation. I began to feel worthy of being loved. I began to love and accept myself.

But that transformation did not happen immediate. Actually, it was a gradual, internal voice of *awareness*. I experienced a returning to an innate, original, *knowing* of a never-lost wholeness. That interior journey began once I had begun to call back the myriads of facets of self and soul that I had discarded in my attempts to be other than Truth. I looked directly and honestly at how I had used the power of free will to "see" myself as inadequate and unworthy and thus to fashion countless experiences which proved that to me. The more I gave myself permission to be loved for my true nature, the more innocent and safe I began to feel, *as* myself.

I was not yet aware of it, but I had somehow allowed my soul to find the chink in my heart's self-defensive armor. I had achieved mastery in self-delusion and the energies I had chosen to play out in this incarnation had completely run me. Unbeknown to me, I had now agreed with my soul to become a student of true mastery. I would master the way of the heart, the way of my Reality as Love Itself.

It was not yet a conscious drive, but subconsciously I was already positioning myself to learn to face, to embrace, and to transcend those energies of perceived inadequacy and unworthiness. I would learn to let go of the mind's relentless pursuit of understanding, and instead allow the body, through breath to truly feel those energies where they had resided in my body. I would learn to stop resisting feeling, and would eventually let go of the immense sadness and self loathing that I projected onto others. I would learn to love those constricting energies into a joyous celebration of their existence. After all, they were my creations, in all innocence as a child of God, exercising the freely given potential of free will. But I would no longer allow them to pattern me and my actions. Now I would call back and nurture these stray lambs into the fold of Living Light.

It would be a gradual learning curve, unfolding within almost a decade of studentship, and continuing in a lifelong joy of discovering forgiveness. But it was definitely grace in action, and I was on the way to a celebratory self acceptance.

Segment V

2007 – Present

Apprenticeship in Love's Reality Begins

Chapter Fifteen

Re-membering Dawns

2007 - Present – Rhode Island

No Such Thing as a Mistake - No Eraser Necessary

How did I segue from my own "pigsty keeper" status, conveyed in the opening vignette, which reveals such a morass of spoilage and self-degradation, to emerge into a joyful awareness that now allows me to relish each dawn's heartfelt prayer/practice of growing in Christ Mind?

As in the parable, where *the father ran out to meet his son*, warmly embracing him, I too was graced with God rushing to enfold me. After boxing myself into sixty four years of arrogant disregard for others' perspectives, I admitted to emptiness and confused impotency. I turned toward the divine I knew was within me. That simple gesture of humbly acknowledging my helplessness sluiced open for me the floodgates of the Divine Parent's joyous flow of gifts. As the son had humbly, yet guiltily, decided to return to his father's home, I turned inward in an attempt to find the peace I had once experienced, long before my earthly existence.

Spiritual awakening is not unlike the experience a young child has, in learning to read. Once the child can discern what the printed word reveals, there is no turning back. The child cannot unlearn to read. Whether or not he chooses to grow in applying the skills, opening new, vast worlds of awareness for himself, is entirely his choice. The ability has been claimed; the treasures await discovery. I was again that child. I was opening to renewed spirituality, but I was still in primer stages, still sounding out words, still deciphering.

Butterfly emerging from chrysalis.

Four things occurred in that awakening process, which proved to be my personal version of the parable's sandals, robe, ring, and joyous homecoming celebration that the father gifted his "prodigal" child.

The first incident, the intervention of an unborn child, puzzled me a bit, until I began to grow into an awareness of the flow of energy within Oneness.

- It is not unusual to feel like one is in a womb again, while floating alone in a pool. However, late in July 2007, after retiring from a Hamptons school district, I was at the health club in New York City, early one morning. As I floated alone in the pool, I had the distinct impression that I was within a womb, but it was not my mother's. I was sharing this womb with another being who loved me and who waited for me to notice it. I was flooded with peace. For days afterward, I walked through the noisy streets of Manhattan's West Village with a sense of expansiveness and quiet expectation.

One early evening soon after, I stood on the rooftop of a building near Sixth Avenue and 9th Street and stared downtown at the empty gap in the city skyline where the twin towers, six years before, would have been twinkling with lights like the other buildings. I realized how short life really was, and reached in my pocket to call my daughter, Virginia. She and Donald had been married for five years but Virginia had not expressed any interest in having children. Out of nowhere, I found myself offering to be a "nearby Nana," should she ever decide to get pregnant. That of course, would necessitate my moving to Rhode Island, but I already felt trapped in a dying relationship, and ever the opportunist, I sought a refuge.

Two months later, when Virginia told me she was pregnant. I realized she had conceived shortly before my experience in the pool. I decided right then to move, and I drove up to check out various apartments near them, and to register my car in Rhode Island. They persuaded me however, to move into their large house when Don said, "Look, you're 'low maintenance', and you're my drinking buddy." I spent those intervening months from November to April, 2008, voraciously reading works by a wide range of spiritual writers. Folks as varied as Edgar Cayce, Caroline Myss, James Redfield, Bruce Lipton, Rumi and Hafiz, Neil Douglas-Klotz (Saadi Shakur Chishti), James Twyman, Joyce Hawkes, and Eckhardt Tolle, vied for my attention along with Winnie-the-Pooh, who was the theme for the nursery walls I was painting.

- I became conscious of this first gift from God when, five months after their daughter Audrey was born, (she was indeed the gift in itself), as I sat rocking her against my chest, her heart spoke to me. Startled, I said aloud to her, "That was you in the womb with me, wasn't it?" Her heart voiced to mine, "I called you here to show me my beauty, and I will show you yours." I had never "heart-talked" before, but there was no mistaking this. It was my first inkling of the real flow of miracles and the deep connection in Oneness.

For the next nine years, I had the privilege and joy of living with and caring for these grandchildren, Audrey and Victor, until they were eight and five years of age. Within that time, they each in their own unique way, taught me how to again see with awe and innocence, as a child does. I learned to greet each dawn with excitement and delight for whatever it might hold. I began anew to sing and clap, to laugh, play, and dance. And especially, I learned to accept what is, without clouding it with judgment or fear. I learned to be fully present to any moment's experience.

This occurence proved to be, energetically, the sandals which have guided my feet on the stepping stones across the raging river of my own resistance. I began my trek inward, honestly aching for an awareness of unblemished wholeness. During that time, I also experienced three other extraordinary gifts of grace from this prodigal Divine Parent.

⁊

The second grace-filled gift came as I was falling asleep one evening. Raised as a Catholic, I was taught in childhood that purgatory was an inevitable step after death. This period of fiery torments, aimed at purging me of guilt, instilled in me a fear of dying. I remember as a child of six, feeling betrayed that the gods in my life, those who were authority and order, were fundamentally telling me I was stained and imperfect. I knew I was not blameless, within the daily give and take of family dynamics. But on a deeper, remembered level, I recognized that I was essentially unsullied and pure. I knew, as every child does, before the perception of comparison, contrast, and judgment takes hold in the psyche, that I was incorruptibly innocent.

I questioned why it had to be an authority outside of me who determined "good and bad," when in my heart I saw how and when I myself chose to be unkind or uncooperative. I did not need to have someone outside my own being, determine "good and bad" for me. That inner knowledge cost me. As a child, and into adulthood, I engaged in a guilt-laden sense of furtive defiance. There was so much that was good within the Catholic tradition, and I am so very grateful that my soul chose to take on those aspirations. However, in acquiescing to an overpowering authoritarian belief system, I had laid the groundwork for a lifetime of guilt and unworthiness. It was not time yet for my soul to lead me to an authenticating of the mystery of individual sovereignty. That moment however, was fast approaching, when I would once and forever more, humbly yet proudly claim my birthright. I would step into the power of *knowing* the oneness and equality of the Love from which I had been birthed.

- Before that would happen though, traveling by airplane, or even falling asleep each night always seemed edged in fear. On this night, however, as I drifted towards sleep, I found myself enveloped within a most delicious, all absorbing light, which at the same time, seemed to emanate from within me. It peacefully beckoned me towards a mysterious freedom that I somehow recognized as essentially myself.

- I was blanketed in a joyous love that suffused my very being. Never had I experienced such rapture, and I did not want the light to dim. I wanted to continue following to its source. I *was* its source, and equally, I knew there was no boundary to it. I felt so unconditionally accepted, so innocent, and so completely, inclusively loved, and one with that Love. I experienced Self-Love. I was gifted a self acceptance. The *knowing* of my beauty within, and as, this undivided Love, eludes the form of words, but I do know that I was not afraid to venture within it further. I do have to say that this *knowing* invaded every cell of my body, every shred of sensate experience. Even now, in any circumstance, I can instantly recall bodily on a cellular level, this remembering-feeling. I *know* I am loved unconditionally. I *know* I AM Love and I open myself to being wholly loved by Love.

But at that moment in time, I had to deliberately force myself to leave that heavenly realm, which was within my very earthly body. I had made a commitment to a little baby girl in the nursery next to my room, and I so enjoyed being in her life. Although I did not want to part with this mysterious cradling of my heart and soul, I feared that stepping within any further would somehow require a letting go of the present bond I had with Audrey and her parents. I forced myself to open my eyes. The familiar darkness of my room surrounded me, but I was different. I knew in my mind, body, and soul that I was loved unconditionally. I was relieved that I was not dead, but more thrillingly I realized that I was no longer afraid to die. In fact, I have grown to await that eventual passage with gratitude.

When I mentioned the incident to Virginia, she agitatedly insisted I get myself checked out for sleep apnea. Three weeks later, after spending two nights at the sleep clinic, I was diagnosed as a deep sleeper, and well within the lowest-risk category for sleep apnea. Well, no wonder. I had been divinely gifted a most potent sleep aid: the gut knowledge that I am loved and guiltless, and that my daily unfolding is lovingly celebrated.

I acknowledge this, energetically, as the parable's treasured ring placed upon my finger as a loving reminder that I am never without the funding with which to meet each day's seemingly taxing demands. I have learned to choose, in stressful moments, to recall those moments of God-Self, so completely suffusing each cell of my body that evening. I prayerfully place that gifted ring upon my many-fingered consciousness during each morning's *shalu* or attunement meditation.

The third gift I received was the discovery of the healing modality of Reiki.

- This immersion into "spiritually guided life-force energy," began in 2008. Under the guidance of Joan Maggiacomo who was trained by Caroline Myss in archetypal "soul contracts," I had begun an uncharacteristically truthful exploration into my childhood habits and propensities. Joan thought Reiki would be helpful for me and told me about a Reiki master teacher who planned to attend the same Myss conference as I would be, in Kripalu in the Berkshires that May. I took the level I Reiki course with that gifted teacher, Myra Partyka, and stepped on a jet propelled "spirituality conveyer belt."
- The student of Reiki supposedly learns techniques for enhancing relaxation and wellness, but there is something special about Myra's manner, which sets the stage for a spiritual unfolding. Myra listens, both to Spirit and to each student, truly discerning the undercurrent of meaning couched in each statement or question. She creates a safety net for each person to explore his or her own soul's yearning. While answering questions directly and honestly, Myra also encourages the student to stretch individual boundaries, perhaps constricted by habit or fear. Class level after class level, students leave Myra Partyka's unassuming, humor and light filled instruction with renewed purpose and a deeper awareness of the mystery and gift of being human.

Reiki, under Myra's tutelage, has been the parable's robe for me. As I live the principles outlined by Dr. Mikao Usui, its pioneer, I continue to wrap myself within the folds of compassion and joy. Through the practice of Reiki, on myself and others, I share that comforting, warmly enfolding robe. Reiki seems for me to be a culturally Japanese, yet universal filter through which I can ever more deeply express the Christ View of "love one another."

࠾

The fourth, and presumably not the final, gift of grace from a loving Divine Father running to greet my homecoming is the discovery of the *Way of Mastery.*

- In 2010, Myra, who had become a marvelous friend to me, gave me a book she thought would resonate with me. Within its pages, I found a path to profound metamorphosis, and to heartfelt peace. The penetratingly simple compassion-centered *Way of Mastery* works include the *Way of the Heart*, *Way of Transformation*, and *Way of Knowing.* This body of channeled writings, subsequent letters, meditations, workshops, and eventual website grew from the appearance of Jesus, or in Aramaic, Jeshua ben Joseph, to a man known as Jon Marc Hammer in 1987 in Tacoma, WA. How I scoffed at the idea of Christ appearing to someone. Yet, my soul had presented it to me, and when the writings resonated within my depths, my heart again met Truth. I relented with a spiritually, as well as an emotionally happy, "why not?" It helped me to later read Jon Marc's biographical *The Jeshua Letters,* which shows his own nine-year struggle to accept within himself the reality of what was occurring through and for him.

I had already "softened the rigidity within," myself when I had begun to live and cherish the principles of Reiki. Dr. Usui, the originator of the healing modality, did not have Jesus appearing to him and instructing him to write things down. But the message he received within his soul and shared with the world, in the 1930's and 40's, is the same message channeled through Jon Marc Hammer in the late 80's to the present day: *only Love is real, and love is who we are.* I had come "home" to the all-embracing love of a Divine Parent from whose joyous love it was impossible to separate, but who had allowed me the freedom to perceive myself as separate and distanced.

The awareness of and daily attuning to this loving innocence, has become for me the energetic equivalent to the parable's joyous homecoming celebration ordered by the father for his son who had turned homeward. I had spent freely of my birthright, but had not discerned well how my motives sprang not from love but from fear. I am not judged for this. On the contrary, I am celebrated for exercising the free will with which we all have been gifted. I savored life and pursued its pleasures with celebratory gusto and verve. The father's heavenly household celebrates my sovereignty of choice. It is now my privileged responsibility to mend whatever perceived rifts I created in the fabric of human familial wholeness. I want to share these grace-filled gifts of awareness with all creation. I joyously and gratefully observe, without fear's judgment and comparison, all of my earth brothers' ways of expressing sovereignty, even if my mind and sensitivities tell me it is evil. I revere the harmony within divinity's eternally unfolding potential of Self-Love. I do not question the mystery of free will, by presuming that, "… in this instance, God got it wrong."

- With these four parable-related gifts, a key ingredient in my healing journey began to stir in my loins and chest, my very cells, and throughout my being: the realization that I and I alone am responsible for my choices. I have never been a victim. An inner wisdom, known in the peace of my undisturbed heart, shows me that my innate perfection is balance and Love. I feel that I functioned in illusion and shadow when I identified myself as a body-mind, separate from the Divine and from everything in creation.

- I acted from fear and learned to guard myself. As I gradually learn to let go of this body-mind identity, I default to peace. I learn to feel into every unhappy feeling that pops up and allow it its full course. I honor my body and its cellular memories. But I no longer identify as that body-mind alone. I remove the obstacles to the flow of grace and can now remember innocence. No matter what form of spirituality I embrace, I am christed. I live from the Christ View of Love as my only Reality. I have seen that nothing is outside of me because there is nothing but God. I am that Love of God in human expression. I am not afraid to exclaim to the world, "I am

Love. I am christed. I am the Christ. I am a human who sees all other humans *as* the fullness and the Light of innocent godliness, no matter what packaging each one chooses for the present moment." This is a claiming of my birthright. This is anointed christedness.

- This is what I am in my chosen human form.
- As Pure Mind of God, this is who I AM.

Evolution to Self-Love

There is no "me." There needn't be. All there is, is Love.

Oh, Comforter Within, open the "me" I thought I was. Show me how unaware I really am. Spill me outwards, spew in front of me my sewerage of omissions and overt acts of cruelty and severity. I look at them, grovel in their filth, acknowledge and own them. Lance this festering boil that I've become, putrid with judgmental, excluding elitism. Drain this dream scab and show me that I am always filled with your all- embracing love.

There is no "me." There needn't be. All there is, is Love.

And in this human condition, I ask you, Love that I am, please help me to know the instant I erect a barrier to compassion. Strengthen in me the discretion that is now lax, so I will no longer rush headlong into conversation that belittles another, even disguised as discussion. I allow myself the clarity to see where I still have not forgiven, the fortitude I do not exercise, to reach out in healing embrace, and the joy I recognize, but don't always share. Help me, Love, to love.

There is no "me." There needn't be. All there is, is Love.

Crack my hardness; dig out the meat of my goodness, encased in the brittle walnut shell of ego. Encourage me to ravenously gobble up, savor, and spit out the bitter shards of this protective casing I've used to hide my vulnerable succulence.

Then I firmly taste the luscious, earthy Truth of me: I savor Love

There is no "me." There needn't be. All there is, is Love.

Celebrating the Prodigal

Reflection

Jeshua's story of the prodigal mirrors my own life's odyssey, adrift in distractedness and forgetting to laugh. After seventy-some years, I gratefully sail into home port on divinely rhythmic tides of joyous awakening. But because I once chose to take myself and my dream of separation seriously, I considered it as quite a drama. Now I see differently and happily join the father's celebration of the prodigal.

In the parable, it is understood that both sons can now engage in the unraveling of identity with blame and unworthiness. The son who has bodily experienced the father's totally loving embrace has come to know the Christ View (not to be confused with the Christian view). He can practice, as Jeshua learned to, a moment-by-moment *choosing to really see* the "other" (even the 'self' outside) as guiltless. With that practice he will be left with no alternative but to accept his own blamelessness. That Christed being comes ever more deeply to know that there is no "other." There is only One Love, One Soul: the *I AM*.

When the dreamer awakes, perceiving grace "from on high," this process of receiving vertically is actually a remembering of the dreamer's own innate higher frequency of pure, innocent beingness and joy. *Yet, it is the horizontal interactions of loving non-judgment among the sons and the entire household, which will bring about true peace.* Living out Jesus' parable, the younger son will now model for his brother the father's joyful, all-enveloping love. And the older will allow himself to receive love, from whatever source it flows, and thus soften into that happiness of wholeness. He will let go of his serious and self-righteous resistance to a childlike, loving inclusion. *Not the mind, but the pulsing Sacred Heart of Humanity, is the axis where these two directionals of grace converge.*

My heart too, is becoming this axis of the convergence of grace. I am beginning to realize that I am both those brothers. Like Jeshua, who daily practiced and grew into his Christedness, I too am practicing to be the Christ. When I remember to joyfully, trustingly keep each and every brother's heart within my own, to see it as my own, I assure the flow of compassion among us all. I am joyfully vigilant to look beyond the persona guises that each person wears and truly see the Truth and Light of each. And in this allowance I discover peace.

The challenge for me now is to choose, moment-by-moment, to stay in awareness of this loving Reality of Oneness. I do not have to be in a monastery or a church, a temple, or a mosque. In the sanctuary of my heart, I can extend Love in the home, the great outdoors, the market, the jobsite, the highways and byways of daily life by remaining in the present moment, facing the person or creature before me and seeing only God-Self. I can practice taking a deep, relaxed breath before I speak, either as an initiator of conversation or as a responder. I can learn to undo lifelong habits of rigid guardedness, and speak words of kind understanding rather than harsh reactivity. I can reach out in loving vulnerability instead of retreating into my constricted, self-protective mode. By returning to my inherent, childlike innocence, I can proffer softness and a receptive joy in my facial gestures, my eye contact and body language. I can begin to check myself against habits of complaint or finger-pointing. I can retrain myself to be the extension of the Love that I am, rather than the judgmental, smug caricature I had put out to the world in front of me.

Jeshua's story shows us how the father models Love's reality and it implies how the sons can receive and apply it. Judgment and second-guessing have no place here. The giving and receiving of Love heals all illusion of separation or "otherness." The dreamer wakes. The Atonement, the at-one-ment, is enacted. The Son remembers to laugh at the joke he has played on himself by thinking he has erred. The son can gladsomely dwell, at rest in the Father/Mother's prodigality of Love and celebrate the child's unquestioning trust that all is well, just as it is.

Unfolding Love's Potential

I trust that the personal vignettes expose what glared at me during my catharsis of honest self inquiry. I saw how each episode, and so many others like it, demanded healing by being *fully felt, explored, and then let go by forgiveness of myself.* I saw that each episode had sprung from an underlying anxiety and confusion. I had desired, and intended to control at any cost. The cost was paid by me and by others, human, animal, or environmental.

It seems that we humans try to control whatever we do not basically trust. However, we do not trust because basically, we have projected upon another what we do not trust in ourselves. The mind plays tricks. We loathe ourselves for denying our own beauteous innocence, power, and light. So in this denial, we project upon another this misperception, and then feel free to judge them for "displaying" what we do not like about ourselves. Evidently, in my desperate need for approval, I did not trust people or things to think me worthy of their approval. Oh what a joke I played on myself.

The glimpses and stories are told, not for their sake but as an owning of the moments I was bereft of sensitivity, brutish in my need to be right at any cost. I was at war with "the other," obtuse and unaware, not only of mine but of each and every being's beauteous power and Light. I was profoundly identified as a body-mind, nothing more. With only a dim awareness of inherent spirit and of God-Self, I attacked first and breathed afterward.

I invite you to the path of the Heart. It goes nowhere but into the comforting depths of who we truly are. We are the inestimably powerful, unconditionally loved, loving, and lovable Mind of the divine parental Source. We are spirits who exist eternally as pure Being, pure Intelligence. This is the Creator's only creation. And in the mysterious prodigality of the gift of free will and individualized sovereignty, we on earth are pure spirits who have chosen to inhabit a human mind-body. We freely choose that path, knowing that as we incarnate, we will quickly forget our essence as pure spirit and become fused with identity as a body, seemingly separate among "others." There will be only echoes of remembrance as spirit but that indwelling wisdom will show itself within the loving kindness nexus of the Heart. When we follow the quiet urges of heartfelt peace, it is a remembering of original innocence. In the indwelling stillness of a peaceful heart we find ourselves within the larger picture, the perfection of Love's strategy.

Extending the Good, the Holy, and the Beautiful

Below are some prayers, practices, and benedictions which helped me to bring light to my shadowed fears. I humbly offer them in the privileged hope of sharing the message of Love. They are tidbits from the workshops, the *Palpable Forgiveness* retreats, the pilgrimages, and Way of the Heart festivals I have been honored to attend. Permission was obtained and credit is given where adaptations were made to others' offerings and insights.

Some are the grace-filled gifts I have received from the Comforter Within and have incorporated into personal daily *Shalu* (attunement) practices. These "pauses that refresh" might be in the mornings with the special vibratory energies of the rising sun, or at moments all day long, in planned or spontaneous inner focusing. Your monastery is your heart. Your ashram is your very presence, in whatever circumstance of each moment.

*"There is a way of breathing that is a shame and a suffocation and there's another way of breathing, a **love breath**, that lets you open infinitely."* ~ *Rumi*

1) **LovesBreath:** Jayem offers explanations and techniques on CDs, downloadable MP3 and PDF versions available through the webstore at <u>www.wayofmastery.com</u>)

2) **LovesBreath:** as it has evolved for me, is a deep yet gentle breathing that focuses on the breath itself and the okayness of whatever is a natural, belly breathing rhythm.

This is a foundational practice. Daily sessions clear the body's cellular memory of its stored pain, sadness, anger, guilt and any possible toxins of personal darkness engendered by DNA, ancestral history, and personal conditioning. This clearing automatically opens the portals of awareness. The body feels expansive, light, and eventually restored to a child's natural joy.

Anatomically, if we allow the lower belly to gently expand outward, that gravitationally allows the guts to sink lower thus allowing the diaphragm to naturally descend, which in turn pulls the breath into the lowest part of the lungs. Although it is the lungs' air sacs which are actually filling with breath, it seems that the abdomen, belly, bones, and limbs are filling too. They are expanding with the naturally increased oxygen flowing to each cell.

The breathing technique is rhythmic, like a baby's natural breathing, deeply, gently entering the body, and naturally emptying. Eventually it becomes evident that we are not *doing* the breathing, but we are *being* breathed. We shift, body and psyche, into an awareness of the cosmically pulsing rhythm of the sacred. The pulse of Love's vibration resounds within our bodies and we organically know Truth, but until we reach a form of stillness, this Truth is drowned out by our egoic distractedness. The body's natural breathing does not lie to us like the ego-mind does.

LovesBreath is how I accessed the forgotten memories and bodily rooted falseness and fear which fueled my life's actions. As I would continue to gently, rhythmically breathe during each session, my mind would eventually relax its guard on my emotions and my body would begin to cellularly recall feelings or snapshots of long-suppressed memories. I *fully* allowed, engaged, felt, acknowledged, honored, and trusted each emotion as it arose. I wailed, screamed, moaned, whimpered, or angrily cursed, always attempting to also return to the breath. Sometimes it would reach orgasmic levels of suffusion. Pain and rapture intermingled. Sadness and bliss vied for attention.

I would try to feel what part of my body most *sensed* the emotion. What was still holding on to the pain or the fear? What organ or section of my body had trapped and claimed the contraction? Most likely, as a child, perhaps up to the age of eight or nine, I had reacted to some form of authority which had trampled my joy, tainted my innocence and instilled or encouraged guilt. It was most likely an unintentional, unthinking action or series of words or habits on the part of the parent or teacher, but it was enough to make me choose to shut down. It was sufficient to form the circumstances to which I would react and trap the child's fear, anger, or sadness. When I located this emotion, I would cradle it, nurture the child's energy, honor it, and release that energy. I would acknowledge honestly that I had returned innumerable times to that trapped energy and had allowed it to relive itself and to spew forth onto others through my own words and actions. I would dig it out and literally breathe light into my darkness. This is how I healed the ancient wounds of my every incarnation. This is how I recognized how I had used fear as a payoff to my insistence that I was separate from my Source. Breathing is the key to freedom.

I did not judge the feeling; I did not analyze it. With a childlike curiosity I allowed it and loved it into exorcism. I knew it as my child's smothered and cloaked innocence alchemically being returned to its pristine beauty within the body that had buried it. This is the union of heaven and earth. This is the coming of "… the Kingdom within." I allowed each emotion full expression and gradually it would subside, having been acknowledged and valued in its bodily-stored existence. Then as I daily did this **LovesBreath**, the episodes of anger, sadness, fear would become lessened in intensity and duration. Breathing would become blissfully peaceful, rhythmic and comforting to the point that I would no longer be doing the breathing but would recognize that I was being breathed by a loving Oneness of which I was an integral aspect.

The daily practice of **LovesBreath** is the proverbial, "meat and potatoes" to my growth in awareness. Without its alchemical transmuting of an ancient sadness harbored within the fibers of my humanity, I easily fall back into forgetfulness. I am habitually distracted from the Truth that as a child of the Divine Parent, living a human life *as* the fullness of Divine potential, I *am* joy, I *am* peace, I *am* Love's pulse and its extension here on earth.

Without the daily practice of **LovesBreath,** I forget to celebrate the message of Jesus' parable. I forget to laugh with the joyfully prodigal freedom that *I am the face of God on earth.*

3) Prayer: (Adapted with permission from the *Sunrise Shalu* of Orie Lightning, heartbuddy, and owner/artist of the **Dragon Tattoo** and its satellite spiritual center, ***Sacred Tattoo Temple,*** in Eindhoven, Netherlands. Thank you, Orie Lightning).

Saying this with slow, heartfelt introspection and visualization, a person gradually steps into and claims the universal birthright to be the Christ.

The person who has joyfully anointed himself or herself with the soothing balm of the Christ View, knows in the heart-gut that despite the pain and drama of the human condition, he or she can still make a habitual choice for love over fear, for joy over seriousness and for cheer (and a cup o' tea) over sadness.

169

No matter what form of spiritual or cultural persuasion that person claims, he or she can exist in a steadily peaceful and loving consciousness. This is Christ Consciousness.

Love-Sharing Prayer (Thank you, Orie Lightning)

Creator/Friend/Cosmos/Brother/Lord,
Take these feet. They're your feet.
May all with whom they walk today, know that it is Christ (Love) who walks with them,
and may they in turn, walk as Christ.

Take these hands. They're your hands.
May all whom they touch today, know that it is Christ (Love) who touches them,
and may they in turn, touch as Christ (Love).

Take this heart. It's your heart.
May all whom it embraces today, know that it is Christ (Love) who embraces them,
and my they in turn, embrace as Christ (Love).

Take this voice. It's your voice.
May all with whom it speaks today, know that it is Christ (Love) who speaks with them,
and may they in turn, speak as Christ (Love).

Take these eyes. They're your eyes.
May all whom they see today, know that it is Christ (Love) who sees them,
and may they in turn, see as Christ (Love).

• PRAYER

I can't fool you, God. I spring from you, AS you. Open me. Breathe into me an awareness of my power, the potential within my seeming fragility.

Infuse me with a knowing that this awe-full power is you, reflected.

I am mysteriously, lovingly individuated, yet in total union with you, joyously, eternally gifted with an essence that flows from you and is me. I honor the reality that without you I do not exist and within you I am all that is.

Help me to forgive myself, in this human psyche for which I opted when I incarnated. Help me to see the impossibility that I am separate from you.

1. *Fill me with the gut-heart grasp of the strength I already have but often refuse to use, so I can correct a judging myself and others, and especially, so I can ask their forgiveness and honor their authentic wholeness. So I can bless them, and myself.*

Let me know within each moment's actions and thoughts, that I do have the fortitude to forsake the rational approach and to grasp the godliness of forgiving. It seems so irrational, this unconditional forgiving of myself and all others.

Help me choose to remember that there is no blame, no reproach, no guilt, because the At-one-ment has already been achieved with my brother Jeshua's fear-conquering love, even unto his dying breath.

Help me to laugh in the face of my false fears because I know that only Love is real.

• *Practice:*

I know in my heart of hearts, I have experienced the biblical, "Ask and you shall receive." (Matthew 7: 7-8) I *have* asked, and I *have* received. **In the very next instant's thought**, the answer comes, the determination infuses … but I don't always honor that thought; most times I second-guess it. At times, I refuse to act on the determination that has imbued my soul with courage. But I do know, and have experienced that the asking does result in the receiving. It is up to me to accept the gift, to utilize it. It is up to me to recognize that the Truth is within me. It is my responsibility to claim the Comforter Within and not wait for a false authority outside of the God-Self. And most importantly, I have learned that it is perfectly okay to not accept the gift of the moment. It is continuously offered by a prodigally loving divine parent who never judges. There is only Love, an abundance of Love.

When I am confused and in the emotional turmoil of fear my mind races non-stop. It loops back on itself. This is the ego's way of being the substitute for God. God is the Truth of my being. The ego is my need to deny that, to fight God as if it were separate from my being. The ego needs dishonesty. I need the world and use it so I can project on it, so I can make "others" the mirror of whatever is not healed, not perceived as whole, in me. My body-mind identity uses the out-of-control mental spinning as a device to continue the dishonesty and denial.

So I begin to heal when I choose to step aside from the mental racetrack. When I begin to be witness to the questions, and observer of the mind as questioner, I can take steps towards love of self, whole self, God-Self. I do this by choosing certain questions that cause a pause. This is a pregnant pause, which gives birth to honesty. I can interrupt the mind's incessant looping and the ego's deceit by asking myself, "Does this thought bring me peace?" or "How does this thought make me feel?" When I take even this slight detour to the racing, I have broken the spiral into the pit of sadness, or opened a valve to the volatile build-up of anxiety. I have taken control by allowing my heart's-truth to speak instead of the mind's egoic clamp on joyful Truth.

"Ask and you shall receive." (Matthew 7: 7-8) But pay attention to the answer. It comes immediately and it comes from the Comforter Within. It comes from you as the One Soul. And it comes always.

- ***Practice:***

Heart of the Christed Heart

I asked Jeshua to help me "get out of my own way."
I asked him to show me, with whatever vibratory frequency I could tolerate, how his Christed heart felt as he went through any given day, meeting person after person. I asked him to pierce the resistance I unconsciously set up to the reality of oneness with everything.
"Whatever you ask for, in my name, I will do." (John 14:13)
It is happening, dear friends of the heart! As a student of the mastery of love's extension here on earth, I am learning to abide more frequently

within the heart's knowing of our infinite FREEDOM OF CHOICE. I am becoming more aware, moment by precious moment, holy relationship by holy relationship, of how Jeshua grew in his heart's knowing.

It takes vigilance ... and diligence. But it's a joyous, child's discovery of innocence. It's a "Pandora the Explora" happiness of the heart, when I open my boxed up, defended heart and I find my beauty that I was so afraid of. It's Sacred Presence with myself in the Silence of the sacred heart of Existence!

Ask, folks! ... but be advised ... it's real! So hold onto your hats; get ready for some spiritual G Force stuff ... in all its lovingly soft, receptive and childlike innocence.

(... and it's not all "up" like this ... but it tides one over when coalesced energy seems to drag one into ennui). I CAN CHOOSE TO KNOW FREEDOM. I CAN CHOOSE TO LOVE ... even in those dense moments.

That is Love's prodigality. That is why I celebrate the prodigal. My soul took me "to where I AM."
Reflection

Aramaic, the language spoken by Jeshua, communicated much like poetry. Words had multiple meanings, depending on the listeners' openness, cultivation of spirit, and world view. Over time, translations into Greek and Latin were done with less built-in flexibility and room for personal receptivity. Subsequent translations into other languages, leave the reader bereft of the richness and depth of personal application that Jeshua's spoken words would have allowed for his Aramaic-speaking listeners.

Importance of an Aramaic understanding of the terms, "*name*," and "Lord."

We read the word, "name," but spoken in Aramaic, it could have denoted *field of influence;* or *atmosphere;* or *spirit;*, or *essence,* among other things. Likewise, the written word, "Lord," could poetically have been used to denote, *a personal sovereignty;* or *an individual sacredness;* or *a self-possessed person;* or *a consciousness;* or *one who knows himself as part of a sacred whole.* In the world view of the Aramaic listener, the word might thus have meant, *every created being, in the Oneness of the Whole. i.e., the God-Self)*

It is in this sense that the following prayers are offered for reflection:

Prayer: (Offered to Jayem by Jeshua, with the suggestion that it be uttered often throughout each day.)

∽

In the Name of the Father,

In the Name of the Son,

In the Name of the Holy Spirit, (Sophia; Shem)

In the Name of the Lord,

<u>***Christ I am.***</u>

I joyfully suggest that you breathe this prayer throughout each day and witness your spirit begin to joyfully soar and your stillness reach new depths of serenity.

In this same sharing flow, I offer another of Jeshua's suggestions to Jayem:

(The word, "Lord," in the heart-knowing Aramaic sense can mean whatever is sovereign.

Since each being in Creation *is* the God-Self, me included, then the word "Lord" can mean every created being.)

Therefore, when I pray/meditate/contemplate/breathe/live/sing this prayer, I am speaking with and of being . . . *as Lord.*

I am speaking to myself and to Self.

How is that for the godliness of ecstatic Self-Love?

∽

I love you, Lord.

I am your beloved.

Love me now.

- *Practices:*

(Adapted from workshops given by Rosie-Maria Love, Senior Teacher of *The Way of Mastery,* otherwise known as *The Pathway).* www. wayofmastery.com

Rosie-Maria Love has also facilitated versions of this process in "Playshops, in conjunction with John Mark Stroud in their "I Am Here" tour throughout Europe www.onewhowakes.org

Catharsis through genuine, embraced feeling of the five basic energies:

THE FIVE STREAMS OF ENERGY.

The intention of this practice is to discover our relationship to each of the basic energies:

Anger, Fear, Sadness, Joy, and Sexual energy, preferably in this order.

FIRST PART OF THE PROCESS:

Each pair sits opposite each other, one being the speaker and the other the listener. Listener remains completely silent, giving full attention without comments. Two minutes is suggested for sharing then you swap around. Each "energy relationship" begins with: "My relationship to (Anger) is …"

It is important that you spontaneously speak about your *relationship* to the energy. **Example:** I hate anger because …, or I love it because … Do not just "story" about what makes you angry.

You continue to explore your relationship to each energy listed above, taking turns to share and not going into any two-way conversations.

When complete you may wish to hug each other, thanking each other in this way rather than going into speaking.

SECOND PART OF THE PROCESS:

The intention is to notice that you can fully get in touch with these energies and know that they *are simply energies*. In themselves they are harmless and only feel bad because we judge and try to suppress them. Eventually the suppression turns into an illness or we end up projecting them onto someone else because we cannot deny them or hold them in any longer. Joy is often suppressed more than any of them. Sexuality has many judgments and connotations of inappropriateness attached to it. When fully expressed in this safe way, and experiencing how easy it is to shift from one to another, you discover the harmlessness in the energy. Many people start to feel less threatened and more ALIVE:

In pairs, you stand opposite to one another and again taking turns, one is the observer. The other one has two minutes to fully allow and feel the energy of (Anger.) This may be shouting, stamping, screaming or other sounds or actions. It can be helpful to think of a time when you were angry, to help you access the energy. If resistance arises and you can't access it then, *"fake it to make it."* Often, this will trigger the impulse and/or memory.

Partner observing: notice how you are feeling when you are in the presence of this energy REMEMBER THAT IT IS ONLY AN ENERGY but allow yourself to feel it.

After expressing each energy, shake the body and swap over so that your partner can fully express it too. Then you will be directed to move onto the next energy.

It is important to end with Joy, then Sexuality, and immediately afterwards you DANCE to some sexually nuanced music followed by some joyful music. Notice how much more alive you feel.

Practices: adapted from the "I Am Here" series of "Playshops" facilitated in Europe and the USA by John Mark Stroud, assisted by Rosie-Maria Love: www.onewhowakes.org

- Maintain an awareness of **Spacious Presence.**
- Follow one's Joy
- Function within a mindfulness of one's "**I Am**" essence
- Quicken an understanding of the messages contained in The Way of Mastery texts by listening and participating in the meditative "deepenings" of the lessons (Found on website: www.onewhowakes.org)
- Actively practice the breathing activity offered and explained by Jayem Hammer in Way of Mastery. www.wayofmastery.com

Epilogue

The Source eternally recognizes Itself. All creation bursts forth as an infinitude of unending splendor and potential. This uncontainable ecstasy of God's Self-Rocognition is the I AM shared fully and equally as my essence.

As a perfect extension of God, I spring from unconditional Love and infinite freedom. It is within this essence, as a sovereign, godly being, that I am graced with free will.

With the power of this prodigal gift, we humans "what if'd" our way to the impossibility of a sense of separation from our Source. Yet free will has imbedded in it Love's Reality. Eventually, this Reality, that I Am Love, will dawn on every human. It's a given. Eventually, every human will surrender to being love, to being loved, to being lovable. Eventually, every human will stop resisting and contracting against its own true nature. Eventually, every human will come Home, unjudged and lovingly celebrated.

I surrendered to this dawning. For more than seventy years I allowed certain energies to run me. Now, I frolic within the Kingdom/Queendom of Love's Reality. I play as the child that I AM, unjudging of myself or of anyone or anything. There is nothing that is not God. Despite whatever seemingly aberrant disguise or fearsome appearance that people choose to mask themselves, they are the I AM. This is the prodigally "insane' gift of free will ceaselessly unfolding and I am humbly in awe of it.

All day long, whenever I can, I drop into the stillness that is within me as the All. This is what Jeshua learned to do and what sustained him in his christedness. I consciously connect with Source and gratefully acknowledge that I dwell there in Spacious Awareness. This renews me, as a knowing innocence, wonder, and joy suffuse my consciousness. Whatever chaos, pain, or excitement may be occurring around me or in my body, in those moments, I can still abide in the world of peace that I create as the God-Self.

Heaven and earth are one within me. Nothing can change the I AM that I have uncovered under the cloaks I have worn throughout this life. I invite you to dwell there in Spacious Presence with me, existing because we are being wholly loved.

Butterfly and bee pollinating flower (Photo by Anthony Brogi)

Printed in the United States
By Bookmasters